Twin Bases
Remembered

A history of Bentwaters & Woodbridge

NORMAN ROSE

W0006494

Twin Bases
Remembered

A history of Bentwaters & Woodbridge

NORMAN ROSE

Woodfield Publishing Ltd

Bognor Regis ~ West Sussex ~ England ~ PO21 5EL

tel 01243 821234 ~ **e/m** info@woodfieldpublishing.co.uk

Interesting and informative books on a variety of subjects

For full details of all our published titles, visit our website at
www.woodfieldpublishing.co.uk

*Dedicated to all the American & British
military & civilian personnel who served
at the Twin Bases over the years*

The badges of the four main squadrons of the 81st Wing USAF that operated from the Twin Bases.

Contents

Park Sims

Foreword

In this book Norman Rose has chronicled a time, a place and an amazing Anglo/American cooperative effort that richly deserves a place in written history. For more than 40 years, from 1951 to 1993, the United States Air Force operated out of the 'Twin Bases' of RAF Bentwaters and RAF Woodbridge, two military flying fields five miles apart in the quiet countryside of rural Suffolk, England, some 75 miles northeast of London. That these bases even existed was virtually unknown outside the local area or beyond those directly involved. Yet for all this time the Twin Bases were home to one of the USAF's most active and premier flying organizations, the 81st Tactical Fighter Wing.

From its arrival in England, the 81st was always an important front-line unit in NATO and the Cold War. At its peak in the 1980s the Wing was the largest in the free world, with some 130 aircraft in six fighter squadrons flying from its two bases in England and four Forward Operating Locations in Germany. As this book makes clear, the Wing flew many different aircraft during its lifetime, but all were supported by a vast array of ground-based personnel, providing everything from aircraft maintenance and logistical support to civil engineering and recreational activities. These many thousands of support people were both military and civilian, American and British, all working together as a team and as a community.

It is from the perspective of civil engineering that Norman Rose tells his story of the Twin Bases, and a fascinating perspective it is, because the story of the Twin Bases is – along with the details of it aircraft, its exploits and its people – also a story of never-ending construction. As Norman explains, when the Americans arrived in 1951 the bases were little more than a neglected collection of corrugated-metal Nissen huts. When they left in 1993 they were state-of-the-art military airfields, complete not only with advanced military buildings and facilities, but also with an entire American community to include roads, housing, shopping, schools and recreational facilities. And Norman Rose was involved in building it all.

My own time at the Twin Bases, eight years from 1978-86, was a longer stay than that of most Americans. From my jobs, first as 'Wing Executive Officer' (Chief of Staff) and then as 'Chief of Morale, Welfare, and Recreation', I knew many of the characters Norman mentions in his book and witnessed many of the construction projects he catalogs. I am staggered at the number of people he remembers and the details of events he recalls. Thanks to his remarkable record, anyone who was at the Twin Bases can read this book and find someone they knew or a project they worked on or benefited from, and probably learn things they never knew at the time.

But my eight years were as nothing. Norman was there for more than 50, first working on the very creation of the bases, then serving in their civil engineering offices, all the while watching them grow and flourish, and finally witnessing their drawdown and closure. There can hardly be anyone better qualified to record the history he gives us.

To set the scene, Norman begins his story with a delightful account of local 'life before Bentwaters', telling us of his childhood in a small village nearby and his first full-time employment as a house servant to the local Lord. Wartime brought the construction of the bases, an invasion of 'foreigners' to this quiet corner of the world, and a new career for the teenage Norman. Starting modestly as a young laborer helping build the bases, he rose steadily through the ranks of the British civil engineering on the bases, until his retirement. Since then he has been a tireless historian of the 'Bentwaters Era' – writing and speaking, organising reunions, making video histories, and acting as a focus for anyone interested in the history of the Twin Bases.

He wrote this book because, as he says: "I wanted to tell my readers about all those nice people I met and worked with over the 50 years since. US military activities in this tiny corner of Suffolk should not go unmentioned..."

Any of those nice people who read this book would be delighted as they share those memories. And the military activities we all contributed to were now recorded here as never before. I'm sure I speak for all of us Americans who served at the Twin Bases when I say, "Thank you Norman, for all you did for us during those many years, and for writing this book. When you were working on the bases, if we needed something done we could always count on you to do it. This book needed writing – and you've done it. Well done."

Park Sims Lt Col USAF (Ret), July 2004

Yours Truly at Bentwaters in the 1950s with my trusty bicycle, essential for getting around the base.

Colonel Jack Baker, the Base Civil Engineer, presents me with a 'Can Do' plaque on my retirement in 1987.

Preface & Acknowledgements

Writing this book was something I always wanted to do in my twilight years. I wanted to write it because the twin bases at Bentwaters and Woodbridge had played such a large part in my life. I grew up in the area where the twin bases would eventually be sited when it was still farmland. I was a teenager in 1942 when construction of the Twin Bases began and was fortunate enough to get a job working there. Little did I realise at the time that this would continue to be my place of employment for the next 50 years! I particularly wanted to tell my readers about all the nice people I met and worked with over that time. I felt that the military activities in this tiny corner of Suffolk during World War II and the Cold War years that followed were worth recording for posterity. I also wanted to record the continuous development of Bentwaters & Woodbridge following the arrival of the USAF in 1951, which was ongoing right up to the closure of the Twin Base complex in 1993.

Most importantly of all I wanted to pay tribute to half a century of cooperation between the local community in Suffolk and their US visitors. Although not without its tensions now and then it was on the whole a harmonious and mutually beneficial relationship which developed over time. Many American servicemen bought wives and families over from the States and rented homes in local towns and villages, becoming part of the local community. Other servicemen acquired British girlfriends, resulting in many Anglo-American marriages over the years.

The bases also provided employment for numerous local businesses and hundreds of local citizens. I was fortunate enough to be one of these and enjoyed a long and enjoyable career working alongside both British and American colleagues. I always found the Americans to be friendly and appreciative and I have many fond memories of working with them.

My grateful thanks go to all those who have given me their most valued help and support and all those who have allowed me to include them in my history of the Twin Bases. Without their contributions this book would have been a good deal less interesting. I must thank Chuck Wrobel, editor of the 81st Association journal *Tailwinds*, who resides in Bayport, Minnesota and was most helpful. Also thanks to Park Sims for his foreword, Stan Pytel for his entertaining chapter about the way the Americans regarded us Brits and our funny ways, Chris Bouwhuis for telling us about his long voyage to reach Bentwaters and Geoff Pleasance for his wonderful painting, used on the front cover. My special thanks also to Linn Barringer for his assistance, especially when I lost my way on the computer. The contacts to whom I was introduced via his website were most invaluable.

My thanks also go to the following people for the photographs included in this book:

Ken Ogden (KO), Chris Bouwhuis (CB), Gp. Capt. Mike Hobson (HB), Jackie Errington (JE), Mary Everest (ME), Stan Pytel (SP), Mason Hier (MS), Freda Cowperthwaitre (FC), Arther Parker (AP), Linn Barringer (LB), Ron Burrell (RB), Chuck Wrobel (CW), Jack Baker (JB), Peter Fletcher (PF), Shaun Toffell (ST), Ron Hastings (RH), Imperial War Museum (IWM), East Anglian Daily Times (EADT), United states Air Force (USAF), Harry Eckes (HE), Geoff Pleasance (GP), Chris Deas (CD), Joe Williams (JW), John Hill (JH) and all those that I have overlooked to mention.

Norman Rose, 2016

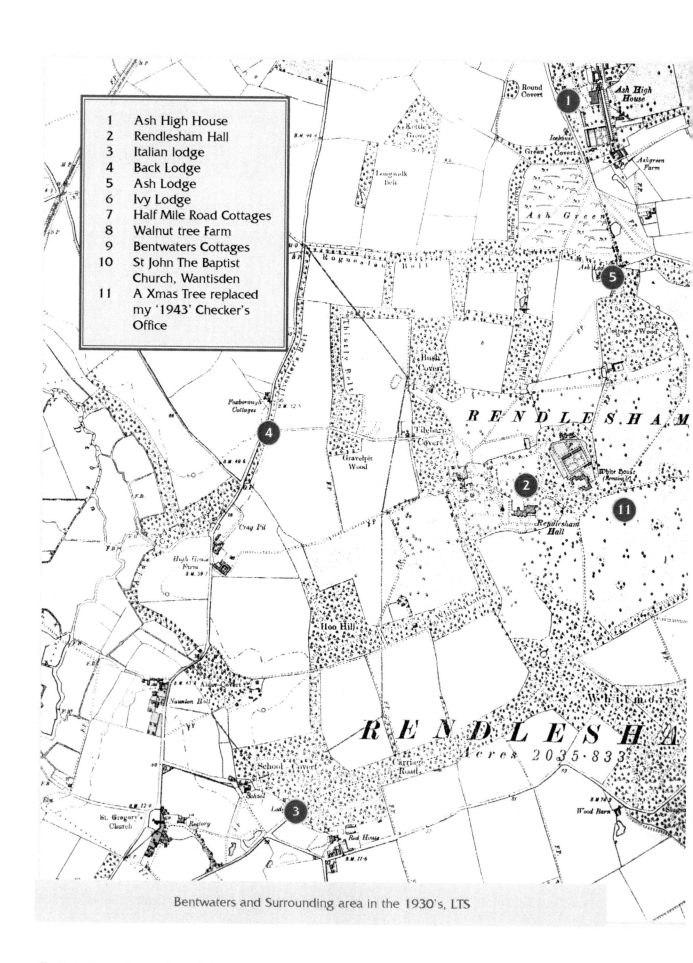

1   Ash High House
2   Rendlesham Hall
3   Italian lodge
4   Back Lodge
5   Ash Lodge
6   Ivy Lodge
7   Half Mile Road Cottages
8   Walnut tree Farm
9   Bentwaters Cottages
10 St John The Baptist
     Church, Wantisden
11 A Xmas Tree replaced
     my '1943' Checker's
     Office

Bentwaters and Surrounding area in the 1930's, LTS

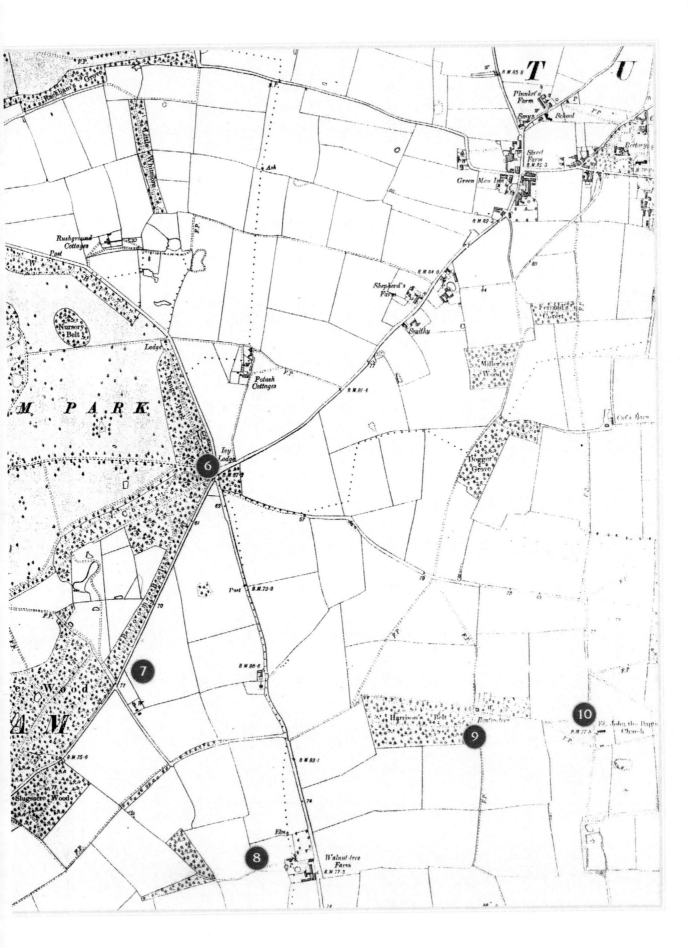

Saint Botolph's Church in the village of Iken, where I was baptised.

My Suffolk Childhood – 1920s/30s

Before I talk about the history of the Twin Bases I want to tell you about my early childhood and the events leading up to 1943, which was when I began to work at, and get involved with the RAF Stations that were created and successfully operated thereafter for fifty years.

In 1926, following the move by my parents from Cockfield, near Bury St. Edmunds in West Suffolk to Iken in East Suffolk, where they were now settled in, I was the first of three boys to be born and baptised in St Boltoph's church on the river Alde.

My first ten years had been a normal childhood for a country lad. My three sisters had now got used to the two-mile walk to school, my eldest sister Olive sharing the sandwiches out to the family in the classroom. My brother Doug and I would also have to get used to this long trek. Harry, the youngest, sadly died of pneumonia at only six weeks old.

Mrs Cooper, the head teacher, was strict but fair. We played in the dirt playground adjacent to the main road which led into the village and had a pleasant view of the river just a field away. Very few schools had a luxury such as a sandy beach, from where we would take swimming lessons and aim for that coveted twenty-five yard certificate.

I remember on one occasion seeing a seaplane land on the river. I was given to understand that it was based at Felixstowe and had chosen Iken for its calmer waters; it was a plane like those competing at the time in the Schneider Trophy.

On another occasion, during the summer of 1938, I remember getting my first glimpse of a RAF low-loader transporter or 'Queen Mary', as they were called in those days. A Gloster Gladiator from Martlesham had crashed near Firs Farm, between Iken and Sudbourne, and it was on a Saturday that the airmen loaded the wreckage onto the very long, low-level flatbed (as we know them today). Towed by a Bedford lorry, the Queen Mary seemed ideal to convey the wreck back to its home base.

Everyone used the village stores, run by Mr Ralph Chambers. This was a halfway stop to school where the family would share out sweets purchased with the refund from returning empty baking powder packets saved by our dear old Mum. The stores also sold paraffin for oil lamps (no electric light at home in those days) and coal for heating and cooking.

The paperboy (who, I was told, originated from Abyssinia – the Italian region) would deliver the dailies to almost every household. Mr Freestone cycled around with a smart attaché case filled with reels of silk and cotton, even shoelaces; most mothers were eager to purchase cotton to repair our clothes.

Ice creams were sold from the three-wheeler freezer box peddled by a young lad, and Mr Vic Last would offer thirteen herrings to anyone willing to spend a shilling; such were the times in the thirties.

Two important annual events stand out in my memory of those special years: The Farm Estate Fête and the Aldeburgh Carnival. Both were held in August or September. The estate owner, Sir Bernard Greenwell at Sudbourne Hall, provided transport consisting of a horse (complete with braided mane and ribbons) and wagon (with those special rubber tyres – very modern in those days) to convey those of us without bicycles – mainly mothers and children. It was also a great day for fathers to exhibit their prize vegetables and flowers and a chance for children to compete in the many races (the three-legged race and the egg and spoon race, to mention but two) followed by refreshments – with the children sitting at a long line of tables on bench seats, to be served with tea from huge teapots.

The other outing was to the Aldeburgh Carnival, a long walk with Mother and little brother across the fields to the river, where we would proceed along the top of the river wall in single file. Made of clay, the wall was very narrow at the top. We would reach the ferry and Mother would hail Jumbo Ward to come in his rowing boat from the Aldeburgh side to treat us to a three-penny boat trip to reach the Aldeburgh main street. Jumbo was always in a dark, rollneck jumper and a jacket with a mariner's badge on the lapel.

One other memorable occasion that stands out when remembering the thirties period was a weekend when a huge crowd of religious folk gathered from all the other villages around. I was a member of the church choir at St Boltoph's in Iken and our little church had been chosen for this special celebration. It was probably to do with the fact that it was the Saint's birthday or something. A large band was playing and men in long robes were swinging brass urns on the end of chains, creating smoke in abundance. It's a strange coincidence that seventy years on I play golf every week with my mate Ken, from Wickham Market, who remembers very well attending that very celebration. Small world?

Our home was a well-constructed semi-detached house down the end of a gravel-surfaced lane. We could see the town of Aldeburgh from the landing window, beyond the many fields and river Alde.

We had nice neighbours, Mr and Mrs George Kersey. George worked at Red House Farm and their son Nat worked as a cowman at Poplar Farm (now known as Stanny Farm). I remember Mrs Kersey standing at the gate watching anxiously as Nat led the massive bull on its exercises. She was always fearful of what might happen if the beast turned nasty but Nat had him on a pole fixed to a nose ring should he misbehave.

A few yards walk beyond our large garden was an overgrown sandpit, a haven for wildlife such as rabbits and an assortment of birds hatching their young. Blackberries were a favourite between meals and I recall reaching for that extra special big one, trying not to disturb a thrush as she sat, but she eventually flew off to expose her lovely blue, black-speckled eggs. What memories!

In 1940 Iken was chosen, along with Sudbourne, to become a Ministry of Defence practice battle training area. It meant a mass evacuation of all the families to other inland villages such as Tunstall, Blaxhall, Snape and as far away as Framlingham – not to mention the horses, sheep and scores of cattle. Such

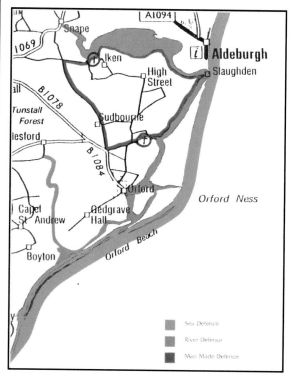

was the upheaval that it was obvious that most of the old folk being uprooted would not be returning to their original homes after the war was over.

Thinking about it now, this was a perfect area for training the military, with the river Alde protecting Iken on the north boundary and extending from Orford to the east of Sudbourne, there was only the one stretch to be fenced the edge of the road Sudbourne to the boundary of Snape. The public was not allowed to enter the area but sadly Mr Chester Richards was killed by a stray shell as he was loading cattle onto his cattle float on the marshes just outside the danger zone at Sudbourne; a nasty accident that should never have happened.

Our family moved to Tunstall and we were now a smaller family as my three sisters had all found work in private service that provided them with live-in accommodation. A number of 'gentry' (as we called them) employed live-in servants, particularly at Aldeburgh and Thorpeness. It was Mother who got the children their jobs, as Father was either not bothered or incapable of knowing what to do in that regard.

Tunstall was quite a busy village. Most of the menfolk worked on the seven farms in the immediate area. There were seven shops, including a wool shop. The Aldus shop baked the bread and provided the Sunday joint. Mr Ted Barnes ran the Post Office and a cycle spares workshop. He also recharged the accumulators to power our valve radio and stocked the other essential grid bias and H/T batteries[1] – costing a staggering 19 shillings to replace. The radio was sometimes silent for a week or two until mother could save up the 19 shillings. The largest grocery shop was Herring's Stores.

Other businesses in the village included a tailor's, owned by Mr Hammond; Mr Balls was the undertaker and the Girling family, as well as selling groceries, managed a small café and

traded in motor fuel. One was not expected to be in a rush should you require a tank fill-up. Mrs Girling would appear with keys to unlock the front of the pump to reveal a handle, which she would turn laboriously to serve exactly one gallon of fuel at the stop point on the dial. She would then ensure that the hose emptied all its contents into the fuel tank of the car – and repeat the process as necessary.

The year 1940 saw evacuees arriving in big numbers and every family was expected to take one or more into their home. A boy named John joined us. He was a ten years old and from Forest Gate in London. His parents were so appreciative of us taking John in that they took the three of us boys up to London to spend the Xmas 1940 in Johns home. This was not really allowed (young children in the capital during this dangerous time) but we got away with it.

Eleven-year-olds from the surrounding villages were given the opportunity to go to the secondary school at Wickham Market, where we would be issued with a cycle, capes and leggings, which all seemed too good to miss. Most of us braved the elements, bearing in mind that the cycles were for school use only. None of us would ever forget the day a German bomber came over the school to discharge its bomb load onto the row of houses at the bottom of the hill, a day when we all took more dislike to this horrible war.

On reaching the age of twelve I was beginning to feel that I would take up any opportunity of work that was going to gain a little independence, especially as we were going to London for Xmas with our evacuee John. The local farms were always a good bet to pick up the odd bob or two. Dick Hambling set me to work with Henry Durrant down at Potash, leading the horse to hoe the sugar beet. It was a lovely July day in the Battle of Britain summer of 1940 and because of the clear blue sky we had a good view of the air battle that suddenly drew our attention over in the Felixstowe direction. We

---

[1] Early valve radios required three different batteries to operate.

were so enthralled by this that the horse moved forward and planted his front foot on top of mine so that I was forced to shout out, which Henry thought was not the thing to do. I've had a thick toenail ever since.

Mr Turner at Gables farm, opposite the church, was also very happy to take Tony Kersey and me to help with gathering in the harvest. We would receive one shilling an hour, which would make us well off and provide us with more money than we had ever had in our lives. When the time came around for us to return to school in early September I was surprised when Mr Turner asked me to come as usual on Monday morning next. I started to explain to him what the score was but he assured me that he would square it with the school governor. When Monday came I was shown how to operate the drag rake and Prince, the Suffolk Punch, obeyed my command, so together we gathered up the remaining wheat and barley straw, leaving the fields ready for cultivation.

Another task that I was to work on with the boss was to gather in the mustard sheaves. The idea was to load the trailer from the back to the front, not standing on the sheaves at all, so as not to shell the seed out and lose the valuable produce. It was interesting when I reached the front of the trailer; I had to stand on Prince's backside to complete the load. Prince was very good and did not seem to mind. All was now safely gathered in and, after an extra four weeks on the farm, I reported back to school.

Back at school the usual classes were in full swing and the woodwork class was the one I remember. It was run by Mr Hales and Mr Wilson. A very strict teacher was Mr Wilson; misbehave and a piece of wood would come flying your way. For the next few weeks we would all be making various items for fund raising. One coming to mind was 'Warship Week'. We had a lesson in how to make model gun turrets out of quadrant with headless nails as the guns; all clever classroom teaching. Other out of school occupations to make a few bob included topping up the water tank at the Green Man Pub and 'brushing' for the gentry shoot days.

Cut Knights and I would meet every Monday evening and, with both pairs of hands on the long, village green type water pump, we would put all our efforts into pumping water into the high level storage tank that was located in the roof space of the old pub. No electric pumps in those days, and golly was I pleased to see the tell-tale arrive on the full mark. It would mean that we would now go inside to see the landlord, Harry Parsons, to collect a well-earned half crown (2 shillings and sixpence) and a sit on the stairs to enjoy a free pint of shandy, which went down very well.

Brushing? Well, I did it but did not enjoy it too much. It involved walking all day on a Saturday through fields of wet kale that was taller than me to frighten pheasants into breaking cover in order that they could be shot. It was not very pleasant work. The only nice part came at lunch break – sandwiches and a bottle of beer – but don't tell mother I'm drinking beer at my young age! Nice, though not very sweet...

These 'shoots', as they called them, took place on most of the farms of the Ullswater estate in the villages of Tunstall and Blaxhall. Lord Ullswater, whose residence was Campsea Ashe High House, let these farms out to local farmers, Mr Turner being one of them. His Lordship took the title from the famous lake in Cumberland after serving for sixteen years as speaker of the House of Commons.

James Lowther, as he was before receiving his title, inherited the estate from his father and settled in during the thirties with Lady Ullswater and their son Captain Arthur. The Captain, who never married, had served and was invalided from the services in the First World War. There was also an unmarried daughter, Millie, who preferred to stay in London. The elder son, Christopher William, was married with a family, but sadly died,

High House, Campsea Ashe, where I worked for Lord Ullswater as a Pantry Boy.

leaving his lordship a grandson, John, who would inherit the title. Millie would visit her parents from time to time, accompanied by her Pekinese dogs.

The gamekeeper, Mr Frank Wardley, was aware that I did not like brushing all that much and came to see mother about another job for me. The staff at High House had approached him to see if he could find a suitable boy who might be interested to work in the big house as a pantry boy. After I had given it much thought, and we had all expressed our views, I agreed to give it a go.

The following weekend I would meet Mr Wardley under the courtyard clocktower for him to escort me to the servants entrance door. There I was met by Miss Mabel Jarman, the head parlour maid, who took me along to meet Miss Wilson the head cook and the two parlour maids, whom I had known during my schooldays, who were older than me and had been there a while. Miss Everet, the lady in waiting, was also introduced to me. I felt a little lonely that I was the only boy in the house. So this was 'Upstairs Downstairs'.

My bed was a fold-up job, parked at one end of the pantry, as they called it. This was a large room with black and white checked lino floor covering. At the other end was a log fireplace and an old-fashioned high chair and table. This would be the main work place for the two parlour maids and I, washing and polishing the silver tableware after it had been used upstairs.

After I had exchanged the trays of new hot food behind the screen, I would not see the dinner party. At the table the girls would pull funny faces to try to make me laugh while I was transferring the used silver tureens. I would wash the silverware in a large wooden tub full of hot, soapy water and these would be polished the next day by the girls. I remember that if asparagus had been the main vegetable the night before it would always take the girls that extra time and effort to remove those very bad stains. All silverware was stored in the walk-in safe adjacent to the pantry.

This walk-in safe had a very large, heavy steel door that was secured which I would guard over through the night period in my little single bed, with window alarm bells all in place. I was woken occasionally by the bell as the gale force winds outside rattled the wooden window shutters. A bit scary for a thirteen year old.

On Monday it was back to school after this trial weekend at the 'big house' but I would return the next weekend. Oh well, it had been something different.

I began working full-time at the High House in the spring of 1942, now fourteen years old and expected to earn a living. Among my other duties was to scrub the stone corridor floors; a section each day over three days. We had to take the good with bad.

"Good morning, Mr Culpeck." I was always courteous to my seniors. That's the way one was expected to behave. Mr Culpeck attended to the boiler in the cellar, which heated the hot water. He also carried the fire logs in a basket skip to the large boxes parked in the corridors. He was very hard working. He lived at Rush Ground Cottages and would walk a half mile there and back four times a day.

I was now settling in and enjoying the challenge. Mabel would let me go in the afternoon, sometimes even to pop home. The one important job I must do every day at 2pm was to deliver the chicken food bowl, complete with wooden spoon, to Shrubbery Farm, just across the park. Her ladyship would feed the chickens at 2.30pm. On one occasion I was late and it did not please her ladyship that I had kept her waiting. Mabel was not going to let me forget it either, so I had to be on my guard from then on.

The courtyard clock above the stables kept good time and was a very good timepiece for the staff, particularly the gardeners. There were so many clocks in the big house, mostly eight-day timepieces. Mr Wight the watchmaker, from Wickham Market, would turn up every Friday evening to attend to all the winding-up that was necessary. The clocks were in the corridors and most of the private

rooms, as well as upstairs. The girls, being young and full of mischief, would comment that they had noticed that the clock in Mabel's room seemed to take a long time for Mr Wright to wind up. Mabel would appear, eventually, rather more flushed than usual.

Three workers were particularly important to his lordship: Bob Cairns the groom, Bill Latter the head gardener and Frank Wordley the chauffeur. The grey horse was always so well prepared and turned out for its cross-country exercise. With his lordship mounted, this was a morning that had been chosen to view the estate and meet the outside workforce. His lordship always liked to keep in touch with them.

First a visit to the timber yard to meet Will Hewitt, the estate carpenter, then through the woods by way of the bridleways to meet the Ling family – Abraham Ling and his sons William and Abie. They were the woodmen responsible for the upkeep of all the wooded areas. His lordship might mention that he had spotted a tree down which needed to be cut up and carted to the big house for the fires. This was always a favourite point his lordship would like to make.

In discussion over dinner one evening, his lordship was heard to tell her ladyship and Captain Arthur that to save him getting off his horse to open the field gate he had asked two girls nearby who, being evacuees, had remarked that it would be appropriate if he were to say 'please'. This delighted her ladyship and a smile from the Captain meant they both approved of the girl's remarks. I would know the next day when the grey had been exercised, as the riding boots would be waiting for me in the boot room.

Bill Latter would turn up in the corridor every morning to see his lordship, armed with a buttonhole flower – a carnation or a rose, something always special – for his meeting at 9am. Much discussion would go on, especially in these times of food rationing. Bill would try to keep the head cook Miss Wilson happy with the vegetable supply.

The head cook had a thankless job, juggling the food and was always trying to twist the arm of the travelling salesman from Lawn Stores, a Wickham Market grocery supplier, to bend the rules to make things easier. Sugar was a problem and we each had our one pound jam jar with our name on it, so that everyone had the same. This was ok for me until the sweet of the day was rhubarb. That soon reduced the contents of my sugar jar. To be fair, the cook did help by putting ginger in the fruit, taking the bitterness away.

Frank the chauffeur would be busy cleaning the green and black Austin car. It's fair to say that Frank was a down-to-earth man who believed in calling a spade a spade. He did not like people who thought too much of themselves and the lady-in-waiting was one of them.

On Thursdays his lordship would sit on the bench as a Judge at the Woodbridge courthouse. The car would proceed down the track across the park to the gatehouse to reach the public road. With all gates shut to keep the herd of deer in, it was always important that Mrs Mowson, who lived at the lodge, would open the gates (known as the Lodge Gates) for the car to proceed. Mrs Mowson, feeling a little aggrieved that she had been interrupted in her housework, would always have her eyes closed as the car passed, to lodge her objection.

I was now getting to know the girls, particularly the two parlour maids who I worked so closely with. Each of us had a half day off once a week but must be back in by 10pm. The remaining two of us, after I had delivered the chicken food to Shrubbery Farm, would sit and read or chat. And with one of them I had taken to like this very much, sitting together on an old high-back chair. It was well able to take the two of us, she sitting on my lap, enjoying the occasional kiss and cuddle.

We had discussed and were now even trying to persuade Miss Everet, the lady-in-waiting, to teach us a few dance steps – to waltz and quickstep and join in with the big band sound which was all the rage now, and she has agreed, so we had another interest. The wind-up gramophone was dusted down and the Victor Sylvester 78rpm records put to use and the lino floor got an extra polish to allow us to glide as we learned the dance steps.

To approach the big house for any particular reason needed courage. It was some distance from the public highway and there were the large heavy gates to open and shut. In spite of this, however, a certain Mr Silverstone decided to approach the big house one winter's evening, looking for lodgings. He was employed at Butley aerodrome, a new construction now under way about two miles away, near Rendlesham Hall. I got Mabel to deal with this man. She duly approached his lordship, who eventually agreed that even the big house should be seen to be playing its part in these difficult times.

Mr Silverstone would turn up at 6pm every evening, I would serve his meal and he would retire to the spare room in the roof space. His lordship would decide how much Mr Silverstone would be paying for his stay at the High House. Not a great deal, I suspected.

As it happened, Mr Silverstone was interested in dancing, so I got some help taking the ladies for a spin around the pantry floor, which everyone enjoyed.

A great three months it had been and we were now good enough dancers to go out into the world and enjoy the local village jig, held to raise money for charity. A hut at Campsea Ashe, known as 'The Iron Room', was one venue.

"Sorry Miss Wilson but Mr Silverstone has not turned up. He must be on overtime. And it's a shame because it was a lovely meal, as it always is, and you're right, it can't be kept warm all evening."

Not only was the lodger late, he did not show up for the next two nights, so Mabel made enquiries. The police rang back to say

The Duke of Kent meets air crews at Mildenhall, 1942. [IWM]

that Mr Silverstone was in custody and that they would keep Mabel and every one informed. The very next evening Mr Silverstone turned up at his usual time, to wonder out loud what Miss Wilson was carrying on about. Apparently, she didn't want him in the house and his lordship said, "I am afraid that if my cook doesn't accept that you should stay then you must go".

A few weeks later his lordship was heard to say at the meal table that the lodger, who had been the aerodrome contractor's pay clerk had put up a good fight in court[1] but was sent down for three months for having four dead men on his books. Never a dull moment in the Big House!

It was during the year 1942, with war moving apace, that a very important visitor arrived. His Lordship's grandson, Naval Lieutenant John Lowther, was visiting his grandfather, accompanied by the Duke of

Kent (John was the Duke's equerry). They had with them a chauffeur and a batman. I was really excited to be sharing the boot room with someone in RAF uniform. I had a crush on that lovely blue tunic with brass buttons. He was an LAC (Leading Aircraftsman).

They stayed the night and the following morning they left, with the LAC and the chauffeur in the back seat. I peered through the hedge to get a look. The servants were not allowed around the front of the house and a high hedge separated the servants' area from the main front door. The Duke and John were in the front of the large, green Jaguar and the Duke was at the wheel. They were heading for RAF Mildenhall to talk to the bomber aircrews who had just returned from a bombing mission over occupied Germany.

A few weeks later there was an unusually early telephone call, which, since I was the only one up, I picked up the receiver and answered. A lady's voice instructed me to get Mabel to come to the phone. The instruction

---
[1] His Lordship was not on the bench on this occasion.

to Mabel was, I later learned, to inform his Lordship that a tragic air crash had killed the entire party, before the news was broadcast in the morning radio bulletin. This shocking news meant that Lieutenant John Lowther had left his eight-year-old son, Christopher, to later inherit the title.

There is no doubt that High House, old though it was, provided a comfortable home for all of us who lived and worked there. The well-kept lawns and gardens, which all of us could walk around to admire the flowers and vegetables, were totally enclosed by a high wall, still evident to this day at the road edge at Ash Green, making it something secret and special.

The moat or canal was again something special. There was a small boat with a cord connected to posts either side of the canal, in which one could cross rather than walk all the way around. The park, with its herd of wild deer, was a sight to behold. Steel railings enclosed and secured it. The Dumpling Gates (still in existence) provided another entrance to the public highway (the B1078). Every year end, a deer cull would take place and all the employees would be offered venison as an Xmas treat.

Shrubbery Farm, across the road from the park, reared only the best chickens to provide the house with all the eggs and poultry required. Milk too was provided, by the small herd of Jersey cows. In the twenty or so acres of park, a beautiful avenue of chestnut trees was a feature which the Lowther family had maintained with great care over the years.

Carriageways snaked through the park, leading to the access points to the public road – the B1078 to Tunstall and Blaxhall. One could see the motor vehicle traffic clearly in the east from the High House dining room as it cut through the mile-long avenue of Lime trees known to everyone as 'The Light'. The drawback was the park was not so friendly in the darkness. The girls, when returning from their half day off at ten in the evening, would want their father to escort them all the way back to the clock tower and only then would they feel safe.

This was quite a cycle ride for their Mr Chigwell, who had to return to Butley High Corner after escorting daughters Floe and Margaret back to the big house. I was never escorted. I had to be seen to be brave, although I must confess that I did not hang around as I dodged around the sheep, etc, as they lay sleeping on the carriage drive.

The original Campsea Ash Rectory, I remember, was vacated by the rector for a smaller house on Ash Green and the Rectory itself was taken over by the Land Army girls. These girls came from many different parts of the country and their western and northern dialects and accents were strange to us Suffolk country folk. The girls were to be seen, clad in their uniform of corduroy breeches and green jumpers, going about their daily tasks in the fields of many farms, whatever the weather.

We would twist Mabel's arm to let us go to the village dances. After the upstairs dinner session and all the washing up had been done, the girls and I would get at least two hours in before the last waltz and we would often see the Land Army girls there, making their acquaintances with the troops. I soon became aware that I could dance better with some girls than others. I also enjoyed a hug and a kiss with my favourite as we strolled back across the courtyard from the cycle shed to the servant's door. What a lovely time we had!

The village rector would often visit the big house and chat to the staff about this and that. He did not forget to remind me that it was important to remain abreast of all things connected with the church and my forthcoming confirmation. After much thought, and a little pressure from Mabel, I consented to attending confirmation classes at the old cottage, the Rector's temporary home.

Percy Haddingham (front row centre left) with ATC cadets. I stand behind the Sergeant on the right.

After a few sessions I was ready to attend the confirmation service, which was held in Eyke village church, near Bromeswell. The service was well attended by men and women from all the surrounding villages, who had all been prepared, as I had, to become God's children.

Church services were held in Campsea Ashe church every Sunday morning and attended very regularly by his Lordship, with Mr Wordley doing his chauffeur duties. It was now too far for his lordship to walk and too dangerous with the increasing road traffic on the narrow country roads.

My duties also included laying the servants' meal table and at breakfast time we had to wait for everyone to be present before we could start. A sly smile across the table would be exchanged with my sweetheart and, with Miss Everet now with us, we could proceed with breakfast. I looked forward to another afternoon and another kiss and hug session. Mabel did not seem to mind this sort of

behaviour by two of her staff. Well, let's face it, there was little harm done.

The war years turned up some strange situations. One of the nice things was seeing all the different uniforms. Some of the estate staff had to serve in the armed forces. Bob Cairns, the groom, joined the army. Mrs Baggs, the head housemaid's daughter Joyce joined the WAAFs. But Jessie, the parlour maid, no uniform for her. She was moved to work in the gardens. This move suited the big house; with Jessie in the gardens, she would be available should Mabel take time off. Jessie kept her bedroom and joined us for meals.

I recall a visit one evening by a soldier named George, who had a long session in the staff room with Mabel and others he had known when he served there as a pantry boy, many moons ago. It transpired that George had left in a hurry when a pregnant housemaid declared who the father was. Well there you were; some of us remember what our mothers tell us and some of us don't! It seemed that even Mabel, with her old fashioned way of thinking, was prepared to pop the wine bottle cork and move on. Everyone had a good laugh and accepted that there was a war on and what the heck.

I now had an air cadet's uniform, so I felt that I was in fashion. Take it from me, one was out of place and did not pull the birds during this wartime period if you were not in uniform. I had to lie about my age to join the ATC (Air Training Corps) at Wickham Market. The age to be a cadet was sixteen but our ATC Officer Percy Haddingham (also our school teacher and a very nice man) would waive the rules sometimes, particularly if one looked the right age.

There was another uniform, as far as the High House was concerned, that I had to be aware of. The pantry boy was expected to wear a dark suit in the afternoons. I was asked to go to the tailors – Mr Hammond in Tunstall – and be measured for this two piece suit. I had to surrender twenty six clothing coupons for

this and in return I would get to keep the suit left by the previous incumbent. As it happened to fit me, I didn't think it was a bad deal. After six weeks I had a fitting and a short time later I collected the suit to wear for the afternoons and also those dances that we were now enjoying.

Xmas came and went and I enjoyed receiving gifts from the girls although I was not able to give much in return as the £2 and 10 shillings I received each month did not go very far. To stay in these low paid jobs was proving increasingly difficult and Mabel was aware of the unrest. She would allow me time out in the afternoons and, after delivery of Her Ladyship's chicken food, I was allowed to go home until 5.30pm with all types of little goodies to keep me in the post. But alas, with numerous alternative jobs available in this very busy wartime period, it was inevitable that staff changes were going to happen. My favourite girl gave notice to leave and after a few months I was telling my mother that I would like to get a real man's job.

Another view of the High House at Campsea Ashe.

Artist's Impression of Bentwaters Cottages by A. Maidstone.
I asked a local artist to paint a picture of the cottages as I remember them. The well was actually located in a wooded area some 200 yards from the cottages but we made it closer in order to fit it into the picture and demonstrate the crooked path that led to it – from which the name *Bentwaters* was derived.

Rendlesham Hall in the 1930s.

The Origin of RAF Bentwaters – 1941

It was on one of my half days off and outside a local shop, Herrings Stores, I met Neville Friend, in his pony and cart. This was a small cart with a step and small door at the rear which could carry about four passengers. Neville offered me a ride. He was on his way to a pair of cottages known as Bentwaters Cottages. to collect some remaining bits and pieces of furniture, completing the home move of the Smith and Woolnough families. These families were being moved from the cottages in order to make way for a new aerodrome, which was now a big local talking point. As we went through Peddlers Lane from the White House I was able to get a glimpse of all the work involved in this major construction and the little cart was shaken up as it negotiated the churned-up areas where the new airfield would soon be. So this was where all the activity was taking place and all these extra workmen were putting in their time.

Mother, who was working at the NAAFI at Rendlesham Hall, where the Tank Corps were based, made enquiries with a Mr Mitchell (of Davies Contractors), the site agent. He was using the NAAFI until the new workers canteen for the new aerodrome was up and running. He told Mother that he could offer me a job as a truck checker at the site office.

So there I was, at a very young age, having to pluck up the courage to tell Mabel that I wished to leave in a month's time. All through the month Mabel tried to persuade me to change my mind, often with tears in her eyes but, even though it was difficult, I stuck it out and eventually the end of a long month came around.

I had missed the girl who had left but another girl, Barbara, had proved good company these past few months – after she had suggested that we meet and have the odd hour to kiss and cuddle in the staff room. She was older than me and was nice company, appearing in her little black uniform dress, stocking tops, suspenders and all that. She was very sweet and a good teacher. I was more familiar with her in some respects than I had been with my previous girlfriend, but it was time to move on.

I did not know until the day I was leaving that it was customary for his Lordship to personally hand the final cheque to an employee who was leaving his service. In the corridor he called my name and I moved forward to receive the cheque. His Lordship thanked me for all the work I had done and wished me every success in my new job. I have to say I felt a little guilty after that, especially as there was no one taking my place.

I made a friendly exit and cycled away, hoping I was making the right move. It was up to me now. I was about to get started at what was to become a most popular workplace for many a British worker for the next fifty years, RAF Bentwaters. I was soon introduced to my new boss Mr Mitchell and he put me straight on to Paddy, who I would replace as a checker. Paddy was going back to Southern Ireland. He had worked in the UK for the past six months but must return home in the allotted time to avoid paying tax on his earnings. Such was the way we had to operate. The Irish were our source of extra labour in this wartime period, bearing in

Carriageways leading to Ash Lodge and Ivy Lodge. An Xmas tree stands on the site of my 1943 office.

mind that a lot of our own workforce were in the armed forces.

My office was a small brick building constructed at the carriage drive intersection with Ivy Lodge and Campsea Ashe Lodge, both roads leading to Rendlesham Hall. Paddy had built up a relationship with the army tank corps cookhouse and was getting a cup of 'real sergeant major's tea' two or three times a day, a habit that he said I should carry on with. The movement of tanks across the park was another interesting ongoing daily attraction; they would also be making their way to Iken battle training area through Tunstall, which was now a very busy village.

The main difficulty in building the new aerodrome living accommodation was vehicle access. The only option was to use the existing bridleways that reached the Rendlesham Hall and clear the surrounding wooded areas to make way for the new concrete access roads. The bridleways were too narrow for the big trucks to pass so the instructions to the drivers were to go into the site through Ivy Lodge and out through Campsea Ashe Lodge.

It must be borne in mind that the half mile road leading to Woodbridge was the only means to reach Eyke and beyond (the Bentwaters bypass and roundabout was not opened until early 1960s).

My instructions as a truck checker were to receive deliveries of ballast only from the Benacre Quarry at Lowestoft because there had been problems with concrete made using inferior local ballast. For example Shingle Street ballast, which had been used on other nearby aerodromes, contained a high proportion of seashells, driftwood and silt and had caused the concrete to fail after a very short time.

A typical example was the airfield at Debach, where the USAAF had to move out and operate from Little Walden in Essex for several weeks at the beginning of 1945 so that the concrete runways could be repaired (all due to poor quality concrete break-up and failure as a runway surface) returning to Debach for operations in March of that year. Not the best thing to have to do at the height of a war. Bentwaters would get it right, even though it meant all ballast deliveries would involve a 70-mile round trip.

The new roads were almost complete, as were the huts and it was late 1942/early 1943 when instructions were given to change the name of the station from RAF Butley to RAF Bentwaters. I remember that a lovely redhead office secretary, Miss Black, was given the job of making everyone aware of the change although few people could have known, as I did, that the name Bentwaters came from the pair of cottages that were demolished to make way for the new runway – the very cottages I had visited with my mate Neville a month or two earlier – or that these were known as Bentwaters Cottages because of the crooked path that led to the nearby well.

Sam Forman, when he was a schoolboy, delivered milk in a specially designed can, collecting the milk from Plunckets Farm opposite Tunstall School and walking up Peddler's Lane to the cottages before walking home to Barn Cottages on the Ivy Lodge to Butley road. This road was closed to the public after the airfield had been constructed.

The Ministry Engineer would allow the public to continue crossing from Butley to Campsea Ashe, however, which was a must for those who relied on making a living selling chickens and rabbits at Wickham Market every Monday. Wantisden Church was just outside the new airfield boundary and would escape demolition.

Each day truckloads of ballast kept coming in and it was up to me to send them where I assumed they were needed – and I thought I was getting it right until Paddy Egan came around the corner, shaking his fist at me and threatening that if he did not receive the next load to his site he would you know what? Paddy's gang were on a productivity bonus, so it was vital that they did not run out of material while they were laying the concrete floor to Hangar 45.

Bentwaters airfield 1943, showing the ten Nissen Hut sites.

Mr Mitchell advised me, after a few months working as a checker, that he would not be able to employ me for much longer, so I moved to the landscape contractor En Tout Car Co Ltd to help with seeding the areas adjacent the runways and learnt to operate the different machinery. This was another very interesting job and the open-air life was something I enjoyed, not to mention the appetite that it gave a growing lad.

Experience on earlier airfields constructed in this emergency wartime period had shown that the seed and soil at the edge of the runway were blown away by aircraft movement in the immediate vicinity. At Bentwaters this problem would be overcome by the first 25 yards from the edge of the main runway having turf laid and pegged to overcome any soil erosion. A lovely meadow at Rush Grounds would provide the turf to be lifted and laid to the 1,600-yard east/west runway, which would be the most used by the four-engine bombers destined to be stationed there.

In September 1943, with the airfield construction nearly complete, everyone in Tunstall was surprised to hear that an aircraft had landed at Bentwaters on Sunday at teatime. All we young boys raced towards the new aerodrome to get a glimpse of this new and exciting development. We even raced past the village copper, PC Howard, who had come to to greet the airmen and record the type of aircraft that had been first to land on the new runway. It was a Marauder, based somewhere in Essex, battle damaged and unable to make it back that extra hundred miles. The USAAF, based at either Martlesham or Parham, came to pick up the crew and arranged military police to guard the aircraft until it was repaired and returned to its home base.

The next morning at work my boss was a little disturbed that the Marauder, as it landed with it's undercarriage down, had struck the soil grader that was parked on the undershoot, leaving it unusable. The cast iron wheels that adjusted the height of the blade on the grader

had been snapped off and it was some time before they were replaced.

The Boss's words were, "No grading today, young man. We will have to get on with other things."

The following weekend a Boston Havoc, similar to the Marauder, landed at Bentwaters, also after suffering battle damage. (As you will learn, this unofficial landing of USAAF aircraft became a problem.)

There was no doubt that the aircrews could see the white concrete runways and, with their radios shot up and out of commission, they were endeavouring to get down wherever they could. Bentwaters was about five miles from RAF Woodbridge (known in the war years as RAF Sutton Heath), which was purposely built with wide runways – three strips, each 50 yards wide – for aircraft to land in any type of emergency, but it was rather hidden by the trees all around it. This emergency airfield opened unofficially in the summer of 1943, before it was completed. Sutton Heath would be used extensively by the RAF and USAAF aircraft – except for those who chose Bentwaters because it was spotted by the pilot earlier.

A system known as Fog Intensive Dispersal Operation (FIDO)[1] was used at Sutton Heath through the winter of 1944/45, saving almost 1,200 aircraft, the highest number of saves out of the 15 stations that were fitted with FIDO.

The problem at Bentwaters was getting the airfield complete without anyone being run

---

[1] FIDO was a system whereby petrol was pumped through steel pipes located along the length of the runway and ignited as it sprayed through small pinholes. The resultant sheet of flame raised the temperature sufficiently to lift the fog to approximately 100ft, providing pilots with a view sufficient to land. Only 15 RAF Stations were equipped with this system and returning aircraft whose home bases were fogbound were diverted to land at them. Prior to the introduction of FIDO the only course of action open to crews who were unable to land was to bale out after the pilot had set the doomed aircraft on a course out to sea. However, FIDO consumed a huge amount of fuel – up to 100,000 gallons per hour – making it a very costly though ingenious idea, which saved many lives and aircraft.

USAAF Liberator landing with the assistance of FIDO at RAF Sutton Heath (Woodbridge). [IWM]

down by battle-damaged aircraft. There was the landscaping to complete and the runway needed to be properly drained for the safety of aircraft taking off and landing in those heavy East Coast downpours.

During a short break from the unofficial arrivals we managed to get a great deal of the work done, although there was one incident when a squadron of Thunderbolts flew over on their way back to RAF Martlesham with one of them discharging its external belly fuel tank onto the Bentwaters runway, narrowly missing a gang of workmen. The plane made it back to base OK and fortunately the men escaped serious injury. Three more aircraft landed a few days later; Lightning's P38s – all out of fuel and, as always, very happy to be down.

Another visiting party to arrive at Bentwaters was the US Army – a force of about one hundred with a Major as one of the officers in charge. They pitched tents on Site 4 and moved into some of the completed Nissen huts. The ablutions had been put into service for them. They used the wide areas of the airfield to march and train and I remember they constructed a bridge using some of the

cut down fir trees on site. They made poles the length of a normal pit prop – about three feet long – and, after wiring them together, they mounted the string of poles onto four upright lengths and marched over the top, as if to show that anything was possible. They also did an exercise of flushing out the enemy at the old Bentwaters cottages before they moved on, never to pass this way again.

I have not mentioned much about the village of Butley. It was the nearest village to the south of the new aerodrome and one presumes that is why it was originally called RAF Butley. Between the airfield and Butley were a few houses scattered in the fields including Hall Farm and St John's Wantisden church.

Butley is remembered for one important incident during May 1944 when a German aircraft crashed into the forest on the edge of the village after being intercepted by a Mosquito from RAF Coltishall. The only survivor of the German crew was Willie Schell, who baled out to land in a tree in Mill Lane. He was slightly injured but managed to reach the Post Office in the main street. The Hazelwood family made him a drink and

Willie Schell returns to thank Joyce for her welcome all those years ago.

Willie gave up his revolver onto the kitchen table, grateful that he was alive and safe from the war. When the Police arrived to make him a prisoner of war and prepare for interrogation Willie told his captors there were five crew on the aircraft, which caused alarm, as only three bodies had been recovered at the crash site. A few days later, on a Saturday afternoon, Police Constable Howard, the Tunstall local copper, asked us lads to cycle to the crashed site and search for the fourth member of the crew. After searching high and low the body was found, hanging in its parachute in a high tree nearby, to relief that this missing airman had not got away to carry out spying duties for the enemy.

Fifty-three years later Willie returned, with his grandson, to visit Joyce Hazelwood to thank her again for all the kindness shown all those years ago.

Also in May 1944, I moved on and started a new job with the Air Ministry Works Department. I had hoped to get the job of driving the tractor cutting the airfield grass but Billy Stebbings beat me to it, so instead I

was destined to become a tradesman tasked with the maintenance of the hot and cold water supply and various other duties once the station was occupied. My first payday for the AMWD was on 6th June 1944, the day of the D-Day landings of Allied forces in France.

The Clerk of Works, my new boss, was a temporary incumbent but one to remember. The old cottage vacated by Ernie Kemp, the local fruitier and fishmonger, who moved to Eyke village, was the only building standing when the Ministry Engineer overseeing the aerodrome's construction arrived to commence work, so he had used it for his office and the now the Clerk of Works, on taking up his new position, would run the Maintenance Department from there until his permanent office was ready.

It was a strange arrangement. I would sign for my £2. 10 shillings (£2.50) wages on the wooden lid of the 'copper' in the cottage kitchen. This was a large metal bowl let into a brick surround with a fire grate underneath, which was used to bring water to the boil for washing the week's dirty clothes. When not in use, a wooden lid would cover the top of the boiler for protection and to provide a flat work surface – and this was where we signed for our wages for the next month or two.

This cottage would become of significant importance later. Its location, before the station was sited here, would have been known as 'the top of the half-mile road'. The cottage was now inside the main gate entrance to the airfield, one hundred yards from the public road, with some of Ernie's fruit trees still evident near the cottage and adjacent to the new guardroom. The two cottages had been made to serve as one office block, with the typist on the upstairs floor. It is important to note that foul drainage was not extended across the half-mile road and that all toilets on the airfield side were served by what were known as 'honey buckets'. A contract was issued to the Turner family with one son emptying the toilet buckets and his brother emptying the trash/waste bins.

While we awaited the arrival of the military and for the contractors to complete their clear-up, orders came through to place obstructions on the main runway to deter battle-damaged aircraft from landing and, hopefully, get them to land on the emergency airfield at Sutton Heath (Woodbridge) instead.

The only obstruction materials available were parts of concrete Anderson air raid shelters. We propped these together to make large obstacles which were spaced along the main runway in such a way as to make it obvious (we hoped) to any approaching pilot that the runway was not clear and thus deter him from attempting a landing. We wondered at the time if concrete obstacles on a concrete runway could be seen very well from the air but orders were orders and we would see...

A few days later I had to take a message to a gang of workmen over by the runway intersection about one hundred yards from the Walnut Tree Farm buildings. Charles Brown, the farmer's son, one of my Tunstall schoolmates, had moved out long ago with his family, the airfield having taken all of his father's farmland and buildings (which were left to deteriorate and eventually fall down). While I was talking to the ganger, a shout came from the workmen to watch out. A B24 Liberator aircraft was coming in to land from the West and heading straight for us, clearly intending to put down on the grass, presumably having seen our runway obstructions. The nearer the plane got to us, the more nervous I became and I was about to make a run for it but 'Rat' Bailey (as he was called) said, "Stay where you are. If we all start running all over the place the pilot won't know what to do." The aircraft, now on the grass and approaching us at some speed, slewed around, with one wheel collapsing, and came to rest adjacent to a nearby wooded area. All the crew got out safely and approached us, not expecting us to speak English. They were so lost that they believed they had landed on the continent.

So far so good, but a few days later another battle-damaged aircraft – a B17 Fortress of 96th Bomber Group, based at Snetterton – came in from the same direction but put down on the runway and scattered the Anderson shelter pieces everywhere. Needless to say, after that the B17 was a write-off. After much discussion at the office a few days later we were instructed to remove all obstructions from the runway to give damaged aircraft a clear run in. The RAF supplied a party of firemen and a fire tender plus medics with an ambulance to be on standby for any future emergency landings of battle-damaged aircraft.

Most of the damaged aircraft that landed were dismantled and removed to the nearest USAAF base and I was expected to help out wherever and whenever things required doing until Bentwaters became operational.

In early 1944 Mr Hicks arrived. He was the new Station Engineer, an important position on an operational station, where the electricity supply must be maintained at all times. There was an emergency back-up power plant to supply electric power for the

B17 'Flying Fortress' similar to the one that crashed on the Bentwaters runway. [JH]

airfield lighting and hospital should the main supply fail. Building 147 was the home of the diesel generator installed to deal with such power failures. I was assisting Mr Hicks and Mr Fred Page (the generator operator) one evening because Mr Hicks was not happy with the test run and wanted to do some checks. Standing outside in the dark, the three of us were taken by surprise that, in these hours of darkness and wartime blackout, it suddenly became almost as light as day. Fred and I were puzzled until Mr Hicks said that a FIDO test was taking place at Sutton Heath (later RAF Woodbridge), probably at 'full burn'.

I must tell you about a particular fine, clear day when a Royal Air Force Halifax bomber joined the circuit, towing a Horsa glider. There must have been an arrangement for the control tower to be operating on a green light or similar for this to be possible. The glider was released and began to descend for a landing on the 26-08 runway. The glider, with its nose directed downwards, took a right turn and headed towards the southeast corner of the airfield, but instead of levelling out, as expected, it just nose-dived straight into the ground. The little fire engine rushed to the scene, although there was no fire, but came upon a scene of total devastation. The huge

glider was carrying a jeep and field gun and 13 French paratroopers on a training exercise. The French Paratroops were stationed at Nacton and Rendlesham Hall following the departure of the Tank Corps to the D-Day landings and were training with the glider in preparation for the upcoming airborne landings in Holland. We had not expected our newly-built morgue, situated next to the hospital, to be put to use this early in the history of our new station – but at least we were prepared for this unexpected tragedy.

On one particular evening an enemy aircraft landed at Sutton Heath (no FIDO on this occasion) thinking that it was one of the Dutch airfields. A wrestling match took place between an RAF Warrant Officer and a member of the German crew but with more help from the extra RAF personnel all the Germans were captured, along with their plane – a Ju88G night fighter – which was indeed "some prize", since it carried the latest German radar, Lichtenstein SN-2, which was so effective against RAF bombers.

The Ju88 was flown to Farnborough, where, after examining the German equipment, the boffins devised improved countermeasures against SN-2 to be used by Bomber Command, beginning with a raid on

Kiel in July 1944, followed by many more bombing missions.

News came in that Bentwaters, although built as a Class A Bomber Station for the USAAF, would not now be required and would be placed on Care and Maintenance until a decision is made about its future. RAF at Sutton Heath, 5 miles from Bentwaters, needed accommodation for their team of aircraft fitters, who were now numbering in the dozens to meet the need to repair battle-damaged aircraft. The small contingent of US Army personnel who had used Site 4 were now gone and with the ablutions in operation this was ideal for the RAF ground crews. The airmen were issued with cycles and as many as 25 airmen cycled between the two stations morning and night to get a good night's sleep.

Now with the Army at Rendlsham Hall and the RAF at Site 4, it was time to organise a stage show – to be put on by ENSA, the forces entertainment association. The newly completed Sergeants mess at Bentwaters was to be the venue for this special show for all the service personnel.

Since I was working for the Ministry I was entitled to two tickets for this one-night show. My sister Doris who was in the WAAFs but at home on leave was happy to go along with me and we sat among the airmen to enjoy the show. Would you believe it? Doris sat next to

an airman who she had known while stationed at Waddington a few months earlier. After the show I waited a few yards up the road while Doris made arrangements to meet this airman, whose name was Ken, in the future. Ken was posted overseas quite soon afterwards but he and Doris were married a few months later. I remember that Curly, an airman working at Sutton Heath with Ken, was to be Best Man but the wedding had to be arranged for a time when Curly was not playing football. He was a professional with Brighton & Hove Albion and football was as important then as it is now!

Richard Hunt, an airman stationed with Ken and Curly at that time writes:

"I served in the RAF for the last four years of the Second World War as an airframe fitter and was at RAF Woodbridge (formerly RAF Sutton Heath) for the whole of 1944. I remember the German aircraft landing there, although I did not see it happen as it was during the night, when we were in our billets at Bentwaters. We were issued with bicycles and had to cycle between Bentwaters and Woodbridge through the woods morning and evening. I was a member of No.54 Maintenance Unit at the time, repairing Lancaster and Stirling bombers, and we saw some spectacular sights at times with aircraft

A German Ju88 aircraft lands at RAF Sutton Heath (Woodbridge) by mistake in 1944. [IWM]

coming in to land with large parts of the fuselage, wings, etc, shot away. How the pilots managed to get them down was sometimes a miracle. I was posted from there in early 1945 to the Gold Coast (now Ghana) West Africa, so I don't know what happened there after that."

Thanks Richard.

So now we know where Ken, the newly-married airman (my new brother-in-law) went after that quickly arranged wedding.

A few months later, in October 1944, there was a marked increase in the number of airman moving around Bentwaters. It had been decided that the new station would become a part of 11 Fighter Group and take up the role of bomber escort for daylight missions over German occupied Europe.

A week or two later I was working with Stanley Adams, a fitter who could turn his hand to anything, on the doors of Aircraft Hanger 45. We had got the doors to open and close properly and were about to leave them in the closed position when an aircraft appeared on the adjoining taxiway, heading for the hangar. There were no airmen in sight and the pilot was indicating that he wanted to continue into the hangar, so Stanley and I don't hesitate and push the doors open to

allow the aircraft, an Airspeed Oxford, to manoeuvre into the hangar and swing around to face outwards before shutting the engines down. Two airmen appeared and stood to attention as the officer pilot, who it now becomes clear is the new Station Commander, taking up his post as the very first of many commanders to serve at Bentwaters.

Although there were no human passengers with the Group Captain, we were surprised to see the airmen lifting a basket down to the hangar floor containing four or five Alsatian puppies with their mother close by, attending to proceedings. The Station Commander would reside in a small brick bungalow that stood on the edge of the public road, adjacent to the officers club. With its own bathroom and an open log fireplace in the small lounge it was modest but comfortable accommodation.

With a station commander in place, it was clear that Bentwaters was gearing up for operations, to join the other nearby RAF stations in the final push for victory. Jackie, a six-foot-plus WAAF officer, was chasing around in her jeep on the airfield while a number of WAAFs in other sections, particularly the dining halls, were settling in ready to get the new facilities working.

The Aircraft Arrive – 1944

It was now 11th December 1944 and everyone on the base who was free to do so had taken up positions from which they could view activities on the airfield. The Woodbridge town fire engines were here, along with the RAF station fire trucks, awaiting the arrival of the first Mark III Mustangs, expected to arrive that afternoon from Andrews Field – a base in Essex previously called Great Saling – named after the late American Lieutenant General Andrews, former commander of the US Pioneer Corps. The Pioneer Corps had arrived at Great Saling on 4th July 1942 and constructed Andrews Field, the first of many stations built by them during the war.

By 3pm a mist was coming over Bentwaters and word got around that the aircraft would not be flying in today, so the fire vehicles were stood down. The next day the first Mustangs arrived, without the Woodbridge Fire engines in attendance, and for the following few days many more Mustangs arrived. I remember how the ground crew, two to each aircraft, met each plane and hitched a lift to show each pilot his parking dispersal.

In all 72 fighters (six Squadrons) were stationed here – 129th, 64th, 118th, 126th, 165th, and 234th – with pilots of all nationalities. They soon settled in and I recall one of them, an Australian, drove an old car with a boot lid that opened up at the rear to reveal two extra seats, which were heavily used by more than the authorised two.

On December 23rd the Mustangs went on their first mission, escorting RAF bomber aircraft on daylight raids over occupied Germany. We had our losses. We heard that Bentwaters lost 8 fighters during the period in which they operated from the station. I used to watch them out and watch them return,

Mark III Mustangs, the type that operated from Bentwaters 1944/45. [IWM]

counting on both occasions but was never sure if any had failed to return, especially when they came back late in the evening. Very exciting, nevertheless. These Mustangs were fitted with the Malcolm-type cockpit hood, unlike the USAAF type that was based at Leiston, which had the bubble-type hood.

I later had the pleasure of speaking to one of the pilots who operated out of Biggin Hill in 1944 in Spitfires and at Bentwaters in 1945 with 126 Squadron flying Mustangs. Flight Lieutenant William Fleming was then in his 80s and living in Durham. William, who was converting from Spitfires to the Mark 3 Mustang, writes:

"The Spitfire was an aircraft with few, if any, vices and one had to be very ham-handed to get into serious trouble. We were appalled, therefore, to read about some of the Mustang's "nasty habits", chief of which was instability and reversibility of controls, which occurred on violent manoeuvring or landing with a full fuselage tank when the centre of gravity of the plane was upset. We therefore viewed the Mustangs with some apprehension.

Flight Lieutenant William Flemming, who flew Mustangs with 126 Squadron from Bentwaters in 1945.

One day when some of us were not flying and were sitting in the dispersal hut, one of the ground crew came in to announce that the first Mustang was on the circuit. We dashed outside and climbed on top of an air raid shelter to watch the silver Mustang land, fearing that all kinds of terrible things would happen to it. It made a perfect approach and three-point landing, taxied up to the Flying Control Tower and out stepped a small, blonde, very attractive ATA girl! We sunk back into the hut with our tails between our legs. With the arrival of more Mustangs we began to familiarize ourselves with the aircraft, and in particular with the cockpits.

Thanks William.

William moved with No 154 Squadron in March 1945 to Hunsdon in Hertfordshire, flying Mustangs IVs, and in April was posted with some of his colleagues to 126 Squadron at RAF Bentwaters.

In March 1945 Sutton Heath was given a break from receiving battle-damaged aircraft and reserved for an important military operation because of its nearness to the coast and its wide runway surface. Operation 'Varsity' would involve many gliders and paratroopers. A fleet of 68 Horsa Gliders would be towed by Halifax Bombers and land to stay overnight, parked on the west end of the wide runway, to take off for the Rhine crossing during the last week of the month.

From the time the gliders arrived we were on a security lockdown; no personnel could leave the station and no visitors were allowed in. It meant that our civilian staff, including Joe Copping and others, had to get messages to their homes via the police to say that they were working overnight or something similar to be sure that news of the imminent operation was not leaked before the gliders, fully laden with paratroopers, left the next day.

The Bentwaters Officers Mess dishwasher was broken again; the balance weight that operated the doors was jamming and was so

Towing aircraft and Horsa gliders ready for Operation *Varsity* at RAF Sutton Heath, March 1945. (IWM)

much trouble, as the chains were continually breaking. Stan was involved in other jobs and told me to go and fix the chains on my own. However, I had noticed that the WAAF operating the dishwasher was something of a film star regarding her looks, so I did not mind fixing the chains, however many visits it would take! There was always a cup of tea when I arrived and I was trying to pluck up the courage to ask her out. My dream was to take this lovely girl to one of my village dances but since I was only 17 and she was 20, I was not having much luck persuading her, so Stan came along with me one morning and said "Give the boy a break!"

She finally consented and on the night of the dance I waited for her on the road that led to the WAAF billets, was feeling over the moon. I would be the envy of all my mates when we arrived at the dance. I waited in the dark wondering 'will she or won't she?' And yes, she did turn up, bless her. She said it had been rather a rush as she was late leaving off work in the kitchen. She said she had dressed so quickly she was not sure if she had got her knickers on or not! We had a lovely time at the dance and I was so proud that I had dated this lovely girl, although I was out of my league so far as knowing how one should behave (it was important to remember what

one's Mum had told one what *not* to do). Nevertheless, it was an evening to remember.

In February 1945 orders arrived from the Air Ministry that 234 Squadron were to move from Bentwaters up to Scotland. The equipment was taken by two Stirling bombers, the bulk of it loaded in the bomb racks of the aircraft. The ground crews were airlifted in an Avro York.

The remaining squadrons continued with operations from Bentwaters. One I recall in particular was the escorting of Mosquito aircraft on a daylight raid on the Gestapo HQ in Copenhagen. Escort operations ceased in early May 1945, with the war in Europe ending on May 8th – with victory celebrations all round.

Bentwaters had played at least a small role in winning the war and was now ready to move on to embrace whatever changes lay ahead. Most of the Mustangs were moved away and made redundant. One or two squadrons were exchanged to fly the new Mark IX Spitfires. By this time we had reached September and important rehearsals were taking place for the forthcoming Battle of Britain flypast. The date had been fixed for the 15th September 1945 and the Spitfires would be the main fighter aircraft to lead on this great occasion over Buckingham Palace.

Supermarine Spitfire IX flown by Douglas Bader over Buckingham Palace in the Battle of Britain Flypast, 1945. (IWM)

Douglas Bader, the now famous legless pilot of the Battle of Britain days, would fly the lead aircraft. Bader, who was now a senior officer, came on the morning of the 15th from North Weald, 11 Group HQ, in his Spitfire to Bentwaters to lead the squadrons from the Suffolk field to be joined by the other squadrons en route. A great occasion.

It was now October 1945 and Bentwaters prepared to join the jet age.

The runways were in need of attention and a directive came through to tar and grit their surfaces. This was done, but not without causing some concern now that jets were scheduled to arrive and operate within the next few weeks. The reason I say this is because a lone Meteor visited the station prior to the squadron arriving and landed on this new surface dressing on runway 02–20. The pilot, having heard the rattle of loose chippings on landing, nervously inspected the underside of the aircraft around the undercarriage, concerned about damage to the complex wheel gear. The old fashioned method of surface treatment was not really suitable for these new jet aircraft.

However, we had to continue with preparations for the arrival of the new aircraft and instructions were given to drain the high-octane fuel from the bulk storage tanks and prepare them for the new jet fuel, called

Kerosene. The remaining few gallons of fuel in the underground tanks would have to be pumped out by hand and the tanks mopped dry, to remove every trace of the old type fuel. The arrival of the new station commander – ex Battle of Britain pilot Wing Commander Laddie Lucas – was seen as something special for the station, which would be the new home of 56 Squadron (previously 124 Squadron) and their Gloster Meteor jet fighters.

Former Battle of Britain pilot 'Laddie' Lucas.

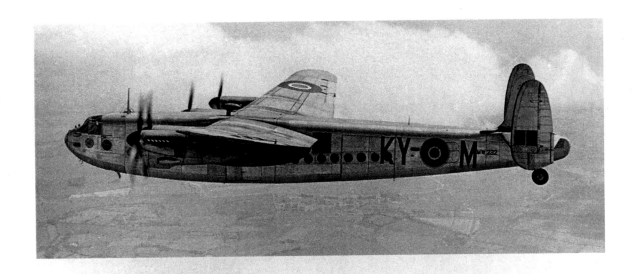

Avro York and Short Stirling aircraft transport 234 Squadron ground crew to Scotland. [IWM]

We had our problems as the pilots learned the new techniques of flying these faster aircraft. The press were quick to remind everyone of the dangers when we lost two valuable pilots in a serious collision. After only one year the Meteors would depart for their new station. The permanent runways were now complete at RAF Wattisham and the Bentwaters Meteors moved off in October 1946. Wattisham was a pre-war station with brick barrack blocks and many more permanent facilities.

Surprisingly, Bentwaters became a conversion unit and continued to be operational for the next three years. No.226 Operational Conversion Unit arrived in a week or so of the Meteors leaving and settled in to train air crews to convert from piston type aircraft to jet power.

Group Capt. Mike Hobson (now retired and living in Woodbridge town) was posted to Bentwaters as a young pilot for jet training and he writes:

"Bentwaters in the late 1940s when, as No. 226 Operational Conversion Unit, it was the sole unit converting RAF pilots onto jet aircraft which were only then beginning to equip all squadrons in Fighter Command. I have a personal interest in this period, for, being a Red Rose man from Lancashire, I set foot in Suffolk on June 5th 1947 for the first time in my life, and was transported from Wickham Market railway station to RAF Bentwaters to start my conversion course onto Meteor Mk.3 jets. That very same evening (52 years ago), I met the girl who was later to become my wife and we have now had a house in Woodbridge for the past 39 years and sent three boys to Woodbridge

RAF Mosquito that swung on landing and undercarriage collapsed, Bentwaters 1948.

School. So I, for one, consider that period of the history of Bentwaters to be quite important enough for a mention!"

The piston aircraft in service were Harvard trainers, Tempest fighters and then onto the Vampire jet. For twin-engine conversion one would fly the Airspeed Oxford and Hornet/Mosquito, moving to the Meteor.

Around the late 1940s German prisoners of war were still retained in the UK and most ex-wartime airfields were used to accommodate these former enemy soldiers, who were put to work clearing up wartime bomb damage.

At Bentwaters at this time the huts at Site 5 were being used to house German prisoners of war awaiting repatriation although the authorities were in no hurry to send these men back to their homeland while there was still cleaning up to be done in Ipswich and other towns where there had been extensive damage caused by German bombs. It's worth mentioning that when the POWs were not at work clearing up they kept themselves busy making models of ships or aircraft which they made to perfection from old wood or metal.

What our station was lacking was married quarters and in 1947 a directive arrived from the Air Ministry Works Department (AMWD) to the effect t they would sanction a contract to convert the tin huts on Site 4 into a form of Married Quarter. Some of the huts would be joined together to make a link corridor to provide three bedrooms. All the huts were to be fitted out with solid fuel fireplaces with a back boiler and a bathroom. The flush toilet would be at the end of the hut in a brick built extension. The huts on this particular site were chosen because they were on the edge of the public road and should the station close down the families would remain in touch with the outside world. The number of married quarters rose to 30, which would be of great benefit to the married NCOs in particular.

By coincidence on 11th May 2003, while I was on duty as a tour guide and chatting with a visitor at the Martlesham Air Traffic Control Tower Museum, I was surprised and delighted when he told me he had been an aircraft engine fitter and served on Hornets at Bentwaters in 1948/9. He remarked how potent they were; an ideal plane to move from piston engine types onto jet flying.

Again we had our crashes. One in particular that comes to mind was a Tempest which came down in the wooded area adjacent the Headquarters site. The crash site is where the bus shelter now stands by the Bentwaters bypass road outside the old Headquarters buildings. Sadly, an unlucky airman who was walking through the wood towards the NAAFI canteen from Headquarters at the time of the crash was killed; I have no record of the pilot's injuries.

I was very fortunate to meet the late Squadron Leader Cyril (Sid) Scorer, who was stationed at Bentwaters in the period 1947/49. His records showed that he had been flying since 1935 on a continuous basis – which unfortunately for Sid meant that they were determined to give him a break and made him Station Adjutant. He was a very good flying instructor and had a great deal of experience in weapons on Mosquitos. Sid flew Bristol Blenheims in the early part of the war and, in common with other Blenheim aircrew, later progressed to the Mosquito. After Sid left the RAF he moved onto civil airlines, completing his flying career in the early 1970s on the passenger Viking Whiskey Delta that can be seen parked at its permanent resting place the IWM Duxford. The Station Commander when Sid was serving at Bentwaters was Wing Commander Knottage.

To prove it's a small world I tell you of a meeting I had at Bentwaters with a trainee pilot who I had previously worked with during my time in the Control Tower at RAF Pershore. A few months earlier I had bid farewell to Tim, who had been killing time with me in the Tower until he went to pilot training school and I went to RAF Manston to work on FIDO. I never expected to see him again after I went back to my civilian job following two years national service in the RAF but I ran into Tim many times – once as he taxied by in his Tempest aircraft.

It was now the summer of 1949 and rumour had it that the station was closing down. What we should remember is that these wartime stations were built to see the war through and certainly not to go beyond five years of occupation. We had, in Suffolk alone, at least twelve pre-war stations with brick built

Hawker Tempest.

permanent barrack blocks as well as all other facilities that were much better and more permanent than those at Bentwaters. With a workforce of 30 in the AMWD, preparations were ongoing to reduce that number by 10 in the first 3 months and by another 10 in the following 3 months. The closure was now under way and the RAF were moving their men to different stations up and down the country, most of them going to Driffield in Yorkshire.

In the autumn of 1949 Bentwaters was put into Care and Maintenance. I was one of the 10 staff who stayed to perform the maintenance. The families were not able to go immediately and one could now see the value of converting the huts on Site 4 into married quarters being by the side of the public road with its bus services, etc. The airman husbands visited at weekends. It was some months before all the quarters became vacant. The barrack warden, Bob Dunnett, and his

The Gloster Meteor became the RAF's first jet aircraft in 1945.

The Daily Telegraph

3 METEOR JET PLANES COLLIDE IN MID-AIR

TWO PILOTS KILLED WHEN PREPARING TO LAND

FROM OUR SPECIAL CORRESPONDENT

6th Jan 1946   EYKE, Suffolk, Tuesday.

Two pilots were killed and a third had a narrow escape when their flight of three jet-propelled R.A.F. Meteor aircraft collided in mid-air over the R.A.F. airfield at Bentwaters, near here, to-day.

One plane crashed into woods skirting the airfield, and exploded on hitting the ground. The second carried on for about three miles, minus its tail, and crash-landed in a district known as Sutton where there is an emergency landing ground.

The pilot died on the way to hospital. The third pilot, whose wing-tip was struck, landed his plane unhurt.

I understand that the aircraft were comparatively near the ground and had "peeled-off" at 1,200 feet to land after a training flight, when the collision took place.

A few people outside the airfield, which is in an isolated part of Suffolk, saw the crash, which took place at about 10.30 a.m. Mr. Norman Rose, who lives near the scene of the accident, said he saw the wing-tip of one plane touch the tail of another.

On the instructions of Fighter Command all R.A.F. personnel were warned not to speak of the occurrence outside their station.

Mid-air collision at low altitudes makes escape by parachute impossible even though the Meteor is fitted with an ejector seat. This has been developed to fling the pilot clear when he touches the control.

The planes were Mark IIIs, a predecessor of the famous Gloster Meteor IV, which won for Britain the world's speed record of 606 m.p.h. last November.

The Gloster Meteor III is a single-seat, low wing all-metal monoplane with a Rolls Royce Derwent engine. It is capable of a speed exceeding 500 m.p.h.

Many R.A.F. fighter pilots not due for early demobilisation are being trained to fly these aircraft, squadrons of which have been formed. The Air Ministry state that the ratio of training mishaps with these aircraft is no higher than with normal propeller-driven machines.

METEOR TESTS

For some months these jet-propelled planes have been going through tests in the Eyke area.

The Station Commander is Wing Cmdr. P. B. Lucas, D.S.O., D.F.C., sporting writer and international golfer, who fought West Fulham as Conservative in the General Election. He is shortly to be demobilised.

The emergency airfield, where the tail-less plane landed, was known to most bomber and fighter pilots who crossed the North Sea to enemy territory during the war as the "Crash Drome." It was the nearest and most accessible landing ground on the East Coast for pilots returning from operations in such difficulty that they could not make their own station. More recently it has been used for demonstrating fog-dispersal.

Sadly, there were numerous crashes involving Meteors like this one at Bentwaters in 1946.

---

assistant Percy Sheperd had been delivering all the supplies of fuel etc, to see that the families would survive a cold winter period.

The last of the airmen left on the last weekend of November 1949, one of them being Ken Ogden, an airman storekeeper who was moving to RAF Wattisham. Ken writes:

"I arrived at Bentwaters late 48/early 49... All I remember is that it was damned cold. As only East Anglia can be cold. Just two of us, straight from trade-training as Equipment Assistants at RAF Credential, Hereford, arrived one dark evening at Wickam Market Station after catching the train from Liverpool St. in London. Luckily some other bods were on their way back to camp and were overjoyed that we were newly posted in as it would mean a truck from camp would pick us up. And they, of course, would get a ride. I came to know Wickam Market station very well... not only from going and coming on and off leave... but also as a despatch point for lots of goods which we packed when the station was closing down.

We reported in at the Guard Room at the Main Gate and from somewhere (I forget) were issued with blankets and taken in the truck in the pitch dark down to Site 5, where a Nissen hut — empty except for wire beds and a stove (unlit) — was to be our billet. The truck driver mentioned 'The Naafi's over there through the trees' and was gone.

Wow... What a welcome. I remember my buddy and me looked at each other and wondered what sort of hell-hole we'd landed in. One memory of the time was that it was so cold when getting up in the mornings that I used to put my hands back under the bedclothes to warm them before I could fold the blankets into the regulation 'square' Over the succeeding weeks we were joined by other miscellaneous bods — fitters, batmen, cooks, and orderlies — a real ragbag of trades, all of

Ken Ogden (front right) with three RAF buddies. [KO]

us waiting for vacancies in our own trade billets.

My place of work was the Equipment Section. You'll probably remember the group of buildings round to the left behind the guardroom as you went through the main gate. Clothing Store, Technical Store and Barrack Store (this had a civilian 'chief'). The main Equipment section office, where all the records were kept and where the Equipment Officer had his office, was between the Tech store and the Barracks store. This is where I worked. The head clerk was a civilian, Bertie Poole, a lovely man, just one front tooth as I remember, but he knew everything about RAF record keeping. You may have known him Norman. He had been on the station 'forever'.

One amusing memory. One day a flight of Meteors arrived which for some reason had to be guarded overnight. 'Volunteers' were required to form a party to guard them and I got picked. (Incidentally, so did my oppo from Vancouver and he remembers the incident well.) Well, our party was split in two to work a 2-hourly shift system and we were to sleep

in a billet attached to the guard room. My shift was from midnight till 2am, so I never went to bed. Straight out on guard (with a wooden truncheon) at midnight. At the end of my shift it was time for bed so I crept into the billet in the dark so as not to waken the other sleepers. Lying down on bed I became conscious of an irregular noise... a sort of, tick... tick... tick. I couldn't get to sleep so decided to switch the lights on to investigate. Wow, it was so creepy. The noise was being caused by earwigs falling from the ceiling and hitting the linoleum floor of the billet. Some, of course, were falling on the beds of the sleepers. I had to get out. Couldn't stay in there another minute. Knowing it was tantamount to suicide waking up sleeping bods, I quietly made my way out and spent the night sleeping in the cab of a nearby kerosene bowser. My oppo remembers having earwigs in his forage cap, so it can't have been a bad dream... UGH!

As far as I know... nothing was ever said about the matter.

Thanks Ken

On the following Monday morning two American Cadillacs turned up and were met by Mr Dunnet the Barrack Warden at the gate house. A number of the car's occupants got out. They were wearing large cowboy hats and all of them were in civilian clothes. Word went around that these Americans were inspecting vacant RAF Stations on behalf of NATO and that they may need at least three for their service personnel in support of an active fighter wing. The feeling was that they would find better stations more suitable in other parts of the country. The Air Ministry had decided to let the local farmers onto the airfield to cultivate the grass areas and grow much-needed wheat. It may be worth pointing out that during the time that we were waiting for the RAF to arrive at the end of 1944 about 12 groundsmen were stone picking. The Forman, Mr Toner Collins, had to think of something for the men to do so, thinking of the gang mowers that would eventually be used, Mr Collins was getting the stones removed to avoid damaging the mower blades. You can imagine those workmen's thoughts when the farmers later moved in to cultivate the airfield for planting corn.

Access was by way of the Butley gate and the Ivy Lodge gate. With the gates now open permanently, the public were back to using the Butley to Campsea Ashe village connection as they had in pre-airfield days. Sunday afternoons were busy, with lots of learner drivers using the runways to perfect their driving skills.

I had been courting Lottie for almost five years now and we had been getting down to house hunting. It was a very bad time to rent a house, particularly if you were not working for a farmer. They seemed to be the only people with cottages to let. But then I thought about how my employer had a pair of cottages and that one of them was vacant; the cottage where I used to get my wages when I first started working for the AMWD. It was surrounded by huts and one end was occupied by the station engineer Mr Toller, who had replaced Mr Hicks when he returned to his home country of Wales. Because the base was now closed, Mr Toller was posted to an operational station (Aldergrove in Northern Ireland). Station Engineers ranked too high to be anywhere other than on an operational station. Only I and the other nine

I am pictured in 1951 outside the cottage at Bentwaters in which I and Lottie lived for 13 years.

industrial workers would remain to care for the station.

My application for the cottage was submitted to Martlesham Heath (our HQ for the AMWD). After a few weeks I received a favourable reply and was told that the rent for the three-bedroom house was twelve shillings a week. I spoke to Mrs Toller, who would be my neighbour, since she could not go with her husband to Aldergrove and she did not have any objections so Lottie and I viewed the old cottage and agreed to sign the agreement. Wedding plans went ahead, Lottie's parents having agreed to the marriage provided we had somewhere to live. In those days it was not the done thing to be married if you had no home of your own to live in. Lottie was one of thirteen; nine brothers seven of whom served throughout the war. I had to admire Lottie's mother and the way she found time to write letters to each serving son in all campaigns from Singapore to Normandy.

Now this old cottage at least had a running water tap over a sink; this was considered something special for a housewife. There was no flush toilet but the contractor I told you about earlier, Mr Turner, would take care of this disposal. It was now May 1950 and after the wedding bells and all that stuff we moved in at precisely midnight that night. The next morning we were up bright and early. My father, Mr Rose Snr, turned up to help me with digging the garden. He complained about the amount of weeds we had to deal with and I remarked it reminded me of the song which was a number one hit at that time – *Just a Rose in a Garden of Weeds*).

As summer moved towards autumn the farmers were preparing to gather in the corn and the station was looking anything but like an airfield, although we had not completely lost all aircraft contact. On the occasional day in the week a target-towing Miles Magister would swoop down low over the airfield and release its target to lie on the grass at the runway edge. He would release up to 3 or 4 of

these targets only to land in the late afternoon to collect them all up and fly back to Wattisham. I was told that target practice for the Wattisham Meteors was ongoing over Orfordness when good weather prevailed.

It was an enjoyable time. Lottie and I had a dog and we would cycle around the perimeter track, catch the odd rabbit and generally love the wide-open spaces the airfield offered us. Our friends would visit us on cycles, which were the main means of transport, and we would all enjoy the freedom from other vehicle traffic. As the winter crept on, darkness was a challenge. To feel happy we made sure that all the doors and windows were secured. The nearest other residential cottages were over a mile away. One night very late I was woken by our neighbour Mrs Toller banging on the partition wall. She was a little scared that two people had managed to get over her garden gate before she shouted out to them to stop right there. We learned later that it was two boys who had absconded from the nearby Hollesley Bay juvenile prison and were looking to get something to eat and drink. These escapees usually surrendered after a few days on the run because of the food and water difficulty.

Life went on and we watched the airfield buildings deteriorate but we could do only the minimum to maintain the security and general upkeep at a given level that funds allowed. Christmas came and everyone went home with a sprig of holly from the two trees in my front garden. I visited the airfield on 6th June 2003 and was delighted to see that the trees were still standing, with new berries forming for the coming season.

In February 1951 suddenly all hell was let lose. W.C. French, the Civil engineering contractor was moving huge construction machinery in and gangs of workmen were working in every area of the station; runway surfaces, industrial buildings and all the tin huts were getting attention.

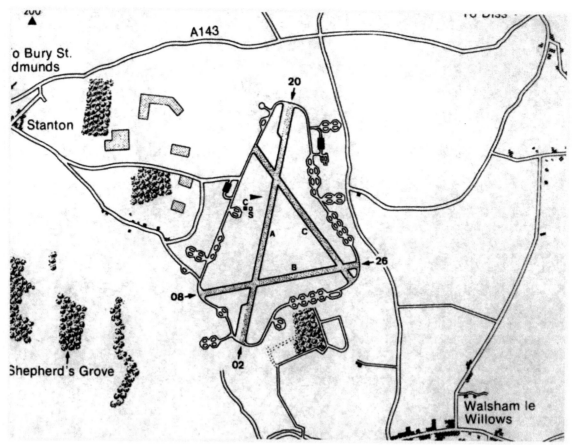

A map of RAF Shepherds Grove where the 78th Squadron was based in the early 1950s. [USAF]

An aerial view of RAF Manston where the 92nd Squadron was based. [USAF]

The Americans Arrive – 1951

Surprisingly the USAF chose Bentwaters to be one of three RAF stations to accommodate the 81st Fighter Wing with their new jet aircraft, the F86 supersonic all-weather support fighter serving NATO. The Cold War era was upon us and the Communist Block countries were to be treated with great caution as they extended from Berlin to Moscow. It was great news that in this mainly agricultural area we would have the opportunity to show what new skills the locals were able to learn and demonstrate to everyone arriving here from across the world.

It would be six months before any operational aircraft or equipment arrived to begin the task of protection or offensive operations. Before that there was a lot of work to be undertaken in a short time to meet the NATO programme. W.C. French had won the contract to refurbish all the huts, to extend the runway 26/08 with readiness pads and lay 'QRA parking ramps' as the Americans called them, at each end of the runway for quick take off.

These NATO stations, it had been agreed, would be shared occupancy, both USAF and RAF. In early summer the first of the RAF arrived. The RAF would total 200 men of all ranks (no WAAFs) under the command of a Group Captain. He and his family would reside in what had been the Station Commander's Quarters adjacent to the Officers' Mess. The RAF were to police the station and liaise with USAF security as far as civilian workers and visitors were concerned. By the time the aircraft arrived everyone was vetted for security and those who did not get through

that vetting procedure could work for the contractor but not the AMWD.

An American advance party arrived in early summer, a squadron of officers and airmen who were not part of the 81st Wing but a detachment of the 7519th Air Base Group who would prepare what they can such as fuel, quality communications, electric supply, etc, and generally work with the British civilian employees to achieve a satisfactory environment for the first trainload of 81st Wing personnel arriving in August or September. The interesting thing for the AMWD staff would be the modern equipment that was to be installed, both electrical and mechanical. One of the most important features would be the modern method of heating the boilers. During the war years coke was the fuel used to fire up the boilers, one to each site for each ablution used by the troops. The water for the three shower blocks on Site 3 was also heated by coke-fired boilers. The airmen's shower block was fitted out with 64 shower heads, making provisions for a mass demand that everyone on their cycle would turn up at the same time. The other two blocks had half that number of showerheads for the NCOs and officers.

All these solid fuel boilers needed round the clock attendance. At the height of a fully operational station and with the steam boilers at each mess hall, the number of stokers in full time work would number over 15, including shift relief stokers. These men were all expected to maintain a high level of professionalism and get the best out of the solid fuel system. It reminds me of the shower block boiler houses and how well and clean the floor areas were maintained and the boilers themselves all nicely dusted down.

Fred looked after all the shower block boilers and when he clocked off at 2pm he remained in one of the boiler houses to cut our hair. It may appear strange to some that us menfolk needed a trim up back and sides in a boiler house, but barbers were a long way from the station and, after all, Fred did have a family of more than ten children to care for, so he was always pleased to earn an extra shilling or two.

A return to operational Bentwaters would mean a more modern and less labour intensive heating and cooking by steam method as we were introduced into automation. The 1950s would see a new type of fuel delivery by means of a rotating spiral auger moving the fuel from a hopper into the centre of a fan assisted boiler without a great deal of manpower or attendance. The number of boilers that one operator could attend to would be far more than previously possible.

District heating was another feature that we would see operating for the three dining halls. One new boiler house would provide the heat to these by way of steel pipes run underground to radiators in each building. The drawback was a certain amount of heat was lost to rainwater surrounding the main pipes if the duct work filled and the drainage became waterlogged. Steam coming through the top of the duct covers indicated a very heavy waste of fuel. Damn it!

The other two stations that the 81st Tactical Fighter Wing used were RAF Shepherds Grove in mid-Suffolk and RAF Manston in Kent. These two stations were also getting a facelift and a fitting out with modern equipment. 81st Wing Headquarters was to be at Bentwaters, which meant that more preparation would be required. USAF Wing HQ stations accommodate up to five Colonels. An American Colonel is equivalent to a Group Captain in the RAF. A Wing in the USAF operates with a Wing Commander, Deputy Wing Commander, Chief of Operations, Base Commander, and Chief of Supplies. These gentlemen all hold the rank of a full Colonel.

The RAF NCOs and airmen took the old Sergeants' mess for their dining hall and the RAF Officers used the Officers Mess as a mixed USAF/ RAF Club. The USAF NCOs and other ranks all used the airmen's dining facilities, a normal practice in the USAF.

It was now early summer and movement restrictions were very much in operation. The access gates had been closed off for some months and many areas of the airfield had been fenced, with security police checking the new passes that we all have been issued with in order to gain access to workplaces to carry out maintenance. This was very strange after having explored everywhere with our dog only a few months previously. Mrs Toller and my wife Lottie and I were able to carry on with our lives. Lottie would not be issued with a pass, she would exit and enter the main gate to go shopping down to Tunstall village or see her family as and when.

Vehicle movement was ongoing 24 hours a day and the numbers of people visiting Bentwaters was growing, with contractors and RAF personnel working together to meet the deadline set for MOD operational requirements.

In August 1951 a small medical group settled into the old large tin hut hospital complex and I found myself attending to minor repairs in off duty hours to mechanical, plumbing and all manner of small jobbing items to keep them happy while major work took place.

The Doctor, a Captain, was so pleased to get these items attended to (he calls in during the off-duty period, which he should not do) but it gave me the chance to earn overtime, so I didn't complain. He did however offer to help me should I need it at any time, which gave me an opportunity to say that my wife was expecting a baby next month and being so far away from the village I could find myself in desperate need for some form of

Unknown USAF airman relaxing outside The Exchange Nissen huts at RAF Shepherds Grove. [CW]

transport. He said he would be only too pleased to help and would await my call.

The airfield at this stage was looking more like airfields should do, with the new concrete pads complete and the landscaping taking shape and a good sweep of the surfaces would make everywhere acceptable for the new jet aircraft. One got the feeling that there was going to be a blitz on all airfield taxi and runway surfaces to eliminate what is called Foreign Object Damage (FOD).

New airfield lighting was being fitted apace, with the construction of brick "B" Centres to accommodate the new switch gear for automatic control.

We at AMWD saw an increase in staff levels and motor vehicles and bicycles. Various items could be loaned from the stores but you would need to sign a loan card and be responsible for their safety. Mr Stanley Hole, the chief storekeeper, was anxious to keep his records up to date. One would sign for a *metal*

file coarse, for the use of (strange terms these storekeepers used).

The upgrading was ongoing at Shepherds Grove at the same pace as at Bentwaters and it had been arranged that the first of the F86 Sabre jet aircraft would go into Shepherds Grove.

Three Squadrons – the 91st the 92nd and the 93rd – were earmarked for the UK but a change was already on the cards. The 93rd would be permanently based at Kirkland NM and the 116th FIS – a Washington Air Guard squadron – would go to the UK as the third squadron of the 81st Wing.

The 91st, 92nd and 93rd had become the 81st Group (Squadrons) way back in 1942 and were ordered to take up duties in the UK in September of that year. They collected their British based aircraft – the Bell P-39 Airacobra – and were immediately sent to North Africa, where they saw action against German and Italian forces. The Group was then transferred to India, where they would take to flying the P-47 Thunderbolt (the Jug). By April 1944 the pilots had now checked out their new aircraft and moved to China, where they engaged the Japanese. Shortages of fuel in China saw a limit to flying by escort fighters and from May 1944 91st and 92nd Squadrons now based at at Kwanghan and Hsian Airfields, engaged in very limited combat action. Col Oliver (Ollie) G. Cellini assumed command of 81st Group on October 24th 1944. He would be the last combat Commander during World War Two. The last 8 months of the war would see the 81st Squadrons enjoy some success in combat operations.

On August 14th the P-47s were called back from their take off. The War was over.

Back to 1951 and the 116th – having now converted from F-51s to F-86As – would depart for the UK in the middle of August. Taking off from Geiger Field, WA on the 13th August led by Colonel Bob Garrigan 81st Group Commander and Lieutenant Col Frank Frost, the 116th Squadron Commander the first leg took them to Hill AFB UT.

It's worth mentioning that the F86 Sabres would make 11 hops to reach Shepherds Grove in the UK. 1st Lieutenant Stewart Stabley, one of the F86 pilots, gives a very good account of the trip made by the first of the F86 squadrons heading for the county of Suffolk.

The Flight from the USA to the UK was to be known as *Fox Able 9 Flight* and it took 14 days for the 116th squadron's 25 aircraft to reach Shepherds Grove. Weather was a main factor with the odd aircraft developing engine trouble. Col Bob Garrigan was the first F-86 Sabre pilot to touch down in the UK. He was greeted by an RAF Air Marshal and the USAF Commander 3rd Air Force at RAF Mildenhall. Everyone was delighted at a job well done.

It was now the end of August 1951 and the sound of jet aircraft over Sheperds Grove and the East Anglian skies would be commonplace for many years to come.

Many of the 81st ground staff were arriving at the two Suffolk stations to take up their posts and settling in their hut accommodation; we call them Nissan huts and the Americans call them Quonset huts.

Chris Bouwhuis, a young airman, gives his version of events as he accompanied the first train load of the 81st Wing personnel on their arrival at Wickham Market station.

SHIPMENT TO ENGLAND

After spending seven days on a troop train across the width of the United States and another week at Camp Kilmer, New Jersey, we were ready to cross the Atlantic. "On or about" August 28th 1951, we again arose early in the morning, packed our bags and carried them to a rail siding. This morning we were heading to the Brooklyn Naval base and the USNS General Maurice E. Rose. I can still remember the very slow movement of the train onto the pier alongside a great, grey hulk. We did not walk up a gangplank but entered through a double door in the side of that greyness. There was no cheering crowd, but there was an Army band playing "So long, it's been good to know you". Thanks a lot!

There is always time in the military for delays. Compartment assignments were made, all bags stowed (Navy term) and then we made our way up to the ship's rail to watch the procedure of leaving the dock. The initial movement was barely perceptible, just a slow drift from the pier. The sounds and the rumblings through the soles of my shoes had not changed. There were a couple of blasts from the ship's horn, an answering toot-toot from a harbour tug and I was sure we were finally underway.

Moving out into the bay, we could see Coney Island and then a green statue of a woman. An old sergeant, Joe Narcy, standing at my elbow said, "Take a good look at her, sonny. It'll be a long time before you see her again."

Another sight in the harbour was that great ship, the Queen Mary. She would pass us somewhere out on the ocean and be in Southampton for three days before we get there.

The rumbling sounds of the ship's engine increased in volume and it would stay at that level for the next seven days. With moist eyes, I watched the USA recede into the haze.

Once out in the Atlantic it became painfully apparent that this great grey hulk was not very large at all. The Rose was a Liberty ship built by Henry Kaiser circa 1943. She (?) was flat-bottomed, not riding well in rough seas. And we would encounter some. I was assigned to compartment C3, below the waterline. Once I put my hand on the outer hull and swore I could feel the cold Atlantic flowing past.

Late that afternoon a Sergeant tracked me down with the news that I had night KP. Damn!

After getting up at zero-dark-thirty I was going to have to be up until the following morning. And I would have night KP every other night during the crossing. Actually, once I found out the benefits of that detail, I enjoyed the experience. I wasn't required to stand in mess lines, I could sleep in the compartment all day if I chose, I had the run of the ship (the GI's part) all night and I had all I wanted to eat at any time, day or night.

One dark rainy midnight the ship was tossing around and the cooks were frying pork chops for the next day. One young cook couldn't handle the smell of frying pork, let alone the tossing ship. His face took on the most vivid green cast I've ever seen. I made a very serendipitous self-discovery; I am not prone to seasickness. I have never been seasick, and I have had some pretty rough rides, ditto airsickness.

The deck space on this tub was very limited for the several hundred enlisted men on board. We had a small 50 by 75 or so area forward and a smaller area to the rear. Some officer with what sounded like a

Some of my AMWD workmates, Heff (with the bicycle) and me sitting it out. Bentwaters, 1951.

This F-86 Sabre flown by pilot Joe Williams is one of the early arrivals in the UK, 1951. [JW]

Norwegian accent was quick on the PA. "Get off the deck equipment." You could sit on the deck, if you could avoid being stepped by a 01 brogan.

One afternoon a group of us were sitting on the deck against a bulkhead where there were open portholes. We heard a voice say, "Hey you men, watch your bad language, there are women in here."

What had we said? Then some guy strolls up with, "hey, what the **** you up to?"

We slowly slink away, trying to melt into the deck plates.

I saw little beauty on the ocean on this trip. The ship was grey, the sky was grey and the sea was grey and I think even the guys started looking grey. Of course the ocean was blue and the sky was blue, but I was bored. Most of us were bored. But I had my night detail and freedom. The ship had, I believe, three movies, one of which was the 1951 version of The Thing. I saw that 'epic' nine times during the crossing.

One evening I was standing as far forward as we could go and saw dolphins pacing the ship, a graceful, beautiful sight. Often flying fish,

tiny ones, were visible 'flying' between the wave crests. A pretty sight.

The 'head' was forward of C-4 in the narrowing bow of the ship. The deck (floor) in there sloped up toward the pointy end. The Johns were little more than seats suspended above a continuously flowing water trough. The showers had three faucets, one for seawater. Instructions on the bulkhead advised the users to shower first with seawater then rinse off with fresh water. I could never get my Palmolive to lather in the salt water.

It seemed like the middle of the cruise when the klaxon horns sounded and the seamen rushed through the ship, closing the water tight doors and dogging them down. I thought, Wow, what's this? A passing sailor said it was 'just routine' and that we were in an area where WWII mines had been reported drifting. Really? I did not think that was 'routine' at all!

Just prior to arriving in England, maybe a day out, we were all lined up at a pay table to exchange our US money for something called 'script'. American troops were not allowed to have US currency in Europe. I had already spent the last of the money I had in the ship's store, buying candy bars, I think. But I did have two pennies left. The exchange officer said it was not necessary to change those. In fact, there was no paper for pennies. The denominations were 5, 10, and 15 cents; one, five and ten dollars. I kept those two pennies the entire time I was in Europe; maybe they were good luck charms.

Finally the ship's engines slowed, the Rose sailed from the English Channel into the Solent, then into Southampton. And there was the Queen Mary! Nudged by tugs against the pier, the rolling and the throbbing of the past seven days were finally ended.

After getting our gear together we had a chance to stand at the rail and watch the English dock workers unload the ship. Their delightful accents drifted up to us and we knew we were in a foreign land. The dock workers had some delightful English profanity too. 'Arse', 'bleeding', 'bugger-all', etc. And something that sounded like "Orff yu Yoint! This was going to be a great experience.

BANG! A new Cadillac, must have been an officer's car, swung on the cable lifting it from the hold and slammed into the side of the ship. I don't believe it hurt the ship, but it did smash in the side of the Cadillac. Now we did hear some scorching English profanity! What a way for an American to begin an overseas tour. A little English train with a toy whistle was awaiting our departure from the ship; it would take us to our new home. The date was September 3rd 1951.

We boarded that funny little English train with its small compartments, each with its own outside door. The train wended its way out of the dock area and north through the countryside to an unknown place called "APO125". England was brilliantly green and you could smell the moisture in the air that kept it that way. Of course all the way across the Atlantic we were in a humid climate. But this place, this England, was different than anything I had seen in my eighteen years in the Western United States.

Along the rail-line were scads of young children in short pants, shouting and waving as we went past. They were holding up two fingers like Churchill's "V for Victory" sign. Someone discovered that the wide leather strap hanging down the door was the device for lowering the window. As the window was dropped to the bottom we could hear the words of those young boys, " Fawk yew yoik!" They did not like us; that was no Victory sign, that was for "You and your mate". We had to laugh. I'm quite sure a few Yank fingers were given in return.

It did not seem that we saw much farm country, not like it was back home. We sped through small town after small town, urban area after urban area. All of the houses appeared small by American standards and were very close together. We sped on through tiny railway stations, the toy whistle tooting merrily as we went past, and crossed narrow roadways, each with a pair of swinging gates on each side of the right-of-way, with a Guard who closed them.

The towns smelled differently too. I would come to learn that it was the soft coal that was used in thousands of fireplaces to heat the English homes.

We must have gone through or past towns and cities I would later come to know, train stations along the way to London and back; Chelmsford, Colchester, Ipswich, Woodbridge and Melton. Somewhere we must have gone through at least part of London; it's hard to avoid on the route from Southampton to where were headed.

At last we slowed and stopped at a small station with a sign that said Wickham Market. It seemed like we were in the middle of nowhere, if there is a nowhere in England called East Anglia. A fleet of American ten-wheel trucks was waiting for us. After

American and British motor cars of all shapes and sizes parked at RAF Shepherds Grove. [CW]

loading our hand luggage, the old awkward duffel and B-4 bags, and ourselves into the trucks we headed out, on the wrong side of the road, down the left hand lane. Crazy! The country road, narrow for an American truck, twisted and turned and eventually deposited us in a place we learned was called RAF Station Bentwaters.

We were left in a sea of bags, surrounded by Quonset huts, corrugated steel buildings with brick wall ends. Our living quarters would be small copies of the big Quonsets, more properly called Nissen huts. But the entire time I was in England we all the huts Quonsets. Only a few buildings were vertically walled box-like structures. The trip had taken us three weeks from the departure by train from Larson AFB in Washington until we arrived at Bentwaters. But FOX ABLE NINE was not complete yet.

Thanks Chris.

The tin huts were confused with what the Americans know as Quonset huts and we call Nissen huts. Quonset huts normally have side windows as opposed to the Nissen hut which have windows at the ends

As Sergeant Howard Gilbert said on a return visit in 2001, it was difficult to remember which hut was yours, but lucky for him he remembered that his hut was under a very large Fir tree on Site 9, the old WAAF site, and its remarkable that the demolition contractors who worked on the old site and tore everything down have left this very tree standing to this day (2004/1/24).

The 6th September 1951 was another memorable day for me, as I will explain. It was midnight and I was in the police post across the road from my home. They were changing shift but I was looking to use the phone to ring my American doctor friend. I hoped he remembered me and would not mind me calling him at this unearthly hour but I was sure he knew that babies only come this time of night, even in America.

He remembered me and the promise he made and asked me "how far apart are they now?" – I not knowing what he was talking about. I said the wife was in a lot of pain and I thought we should be heading for the hospital now. He agreed and told me to stand by; a vehicle would be up to the cottage shortly.

Our neighbour Mrs Toller was good enough to accompany the wife and me and we were treated to a lift in an ambulance unlike any I had seen before. I think the airman driver said it was a Cadillac, which left me feeling honoured and privileged to be the first to use this streamlined ambulance, fitted with all the extras, including a cigar lighter, something new to me in a motor vehicle.

Our daughter was born on the 8th September 1951 and it so happens that her husband Rick was born on the same day. Anyway, after a week of living on my own it was time to collect the wife and little Jenny and be a family again, so off I went to see my American doctor friend again to ask another big favour of him. "It so happens," he said, "that the Colonel (the senior doctor) is going to Ipswich hospital this morning. I would ask him to collect mother and baby and return them to Bentwaters." I did not realise at the time that the Colonel would have to sign for Lottie's ration book when she was transferred; this very important document was one of the necessities of life in the 1950s.

Back in the USA, the Wing Commander for the 81st – Colonel Gladwyn Pinkston – was preparing to lead the other two squadrons – the 91st and 92nd – to the UK by the same route that the 116th squadron had taken previously.

Taking off from Larson Air Force Base, Washington on 11th September it would be 2nd October before 91st Squadron arrived at Bentwaters and 3rd October when Wing Commander Colonel Pinkston landed at Shepherds Grove leading the 92nd.

For the new aircrew and ground staff it would be a while before the shock of arriving at this new base sinks in. As I said earlier, on the airfield side of the public road there were no mod cons and it would be a while before flush toilets were installed in this area due to the sewage works not being large enough to deal with any increase in input.

The first three projects to be considered for planning and construction were a Chapel, a Library and a separate funded (non-military) Rod & Gun Club. The Chapel and Library were still standing on 30th July 2003 – two of the very few original buildings that were requested by the Americans in the early 1950s.

By Autumn 1951 the refurbishing of the old wartime buildings was nearly complete, with one major improvement, the addition of showers fitted to each site ablution, which would benefit the troops, who would not have to cycle to Site 3 every time they feel like indulging in a shower, something that the Americans were used to taking very regularly.

The Cadillac ambulance (centre) that conveyed my expectant wife to Ipswich hospital. [USAF]

It is not long before the roar of jet engines is all too familiar to us all as the Sabres get airborne to familiarise themselves with the Bentwaters circuit and the runway approaches. The dining hall or 'chow hall', as the Americans like to call, it is now a very busy place and, with the emergency programme that everyone would be working to, the chow hall would be operating 24 hours a day to meet the demand of the various shift patterns.

There is a very real need for civilians to work in the dining hall alongside the USAF servicemen and a contract is drawn up for Mr Dutson, assisted by Mr Wragg, to hire and fire these people to tackle the chores of operating the 'clipper' (or dishwasher, as we know it) and clean the pots and pans, tables and floors from 6am to 6pm every day.

As time went on more and more of these types of contracts were issued – to allow the airmen to get down to the military work they were trained for. We have to remember there were no Married Quarters on the station for the wives and children who would be arriving or were already accompanying their service husbands to Bentwaters at this time.

Civilian hotels away from the station would be used to accommodate the wives and families who preferred to be with their spouses. There would also be the occasional house to let, which the American families would be happy to rent and send their children to a local village school. So many options lay ahead for this new invasion that would take Suffolk by storm.

Colonel Pinkston, the Wing Commander, was settling down in his office at Headquarters, known as Site № 1. The Colonel would be the first of 32 Wing Commanders to serve at Bentwaters during the next 42 years occupation by the 81st Tactical Fighter Bomber Wing. Site № 1 also housed the main telephone exchange, with mainly female civilian telephone operators operating this switchboard during the day while the military took over during the night and at weekends; it

would be some time before Bentwaters got an automatic telephone switchboard.

Another section that worked at Site № 1 was the Accounts Section, where the base's finances were controlled from a large tin hut underneath the trees. Always a very busy place. Incidentally, the £/$ exchange rate in 1951 was $3.90 to the £1. I had the pleasure of meeting Mrs Cowperthwaite, formerly Freda Mann, who worked in this building and married her American sweetheart, a member of the 91st Squadron, in 1957. She returned to Bentwaters for the civilian workers reunion in May 2002, when it was a joy to speak with her. She remembers the Accounting Section moving to a very large hangar-type building on the Airfield Technical Site to bring all the clerical types together in one building. She and her new husband moved back to the States in 1958, where she made many friends as they moved across the States to different bases. Sadly, her husband died in 1967 and she returned to live in the UK.

The Nissen huts, which were the airmen's billets, were heated by a solid fuel stove known as a pot-belly stove that stood in the centre of the room. The fuel (coke) was available from a compound on each site. The airmen would take in turns to collect the coke and dispose of the ashes through the week and weekends. This arrangement for heating was not to last very long. A supply of oil and new oil-burner stoves soon arrived from the USA and a self-help programme was arranged through each Squadron to set up oil drums mounted on a support frame at the side of each billet to gravity feed the stove, with the drums refilled by the supply squadron as required – a much better way to keep warm (and not having to rely on a certain individual to get his act together!).

A good deal of the work was performed by the Base Civil Engineer, which was new to those of us who had only dealt with the RAF, who relied on the AMWD to provide all the facilities and services for each building and structure on the station. We would from now

91st Squadron pilots gather for a photocall with a Sabre. [USAF]

on have to get used to the idea of calling the 'station' a 'base', which was the USAF terminology.

The (BCE) Base Civil Engineer had men from a number of trades, involved in various types of alterations and construction work. We noticed the BCE staff getting involved also in the water treatment plant, sewage treatment and roads and pavements. Mr Harry Page, who operated the water plant, was surprised to get an assistant by the name of S/Sgt Kelly who took an interest in the treatment of drinking water that had previously seemed like a daily routine. We have to remember that the American Military was bound to be cautious as they settled in to a strange environment, with the BCE responsible for what would eventually become many hundreds of personnel.

The BCE employed a civilian architect and would be developing a drawing office that would work alongside the AMWD office so that each project would show every detail of the structure as required.

This was another entity that the AMWD would benefit from, the squadron personnel submitting the requirements to the BCE with

the AMWD receiving a first-class, detailed drawing.

The first three projects were with the AMWD, that is the Chapel, Library and Rod & Gun Club, with a construction start date of 1952/53. These three projects were the beginning of scores of projects that would cost millions of pounds, take 42 years to complete and totally change the face of RAF Bentwaters.

What was previously known as the NAAFI would now be known as the 'BX' (Base Exchange) later to become AFEES (Army & Air Force Exchange Service). This would be another busy organisation. The Americans like their doughnuts and coffee, which would be taken around the airfield in the 'chow wagon' as it was known, very similar to the Mobile NAAFI vans of the war years. The old NAAFI complex would be a cafeteria for all ranks, including dependents, as a meeting place, also selling newspapers, magazines, etc.

Adjacent the AFEES would be the Gent's Hairdressers, which would be run by a civilian owner as a private enterprise and would be manned by up to six or more barbers by the time the base gets into full swing.

The officers and the senior NCOs would have their own hairdressing salons. In the late 1950s a chap called Pete ran the Officers' Hairdressers in a small room at the Officers' Club for a number of years.

A military-style 'short back and sides' was the only style on offer.

The British Government and the US Embassy in London set up the Anglo-American Committee in 1952 to promote friendship and understanding between US service personnel and the British communities in which they were living. The committee consisted of eight American and eight British members, with the Wing Commander and a British member serving as joint chairmen.

I have mentioned the increase of traffic around Bentwaters and the surrounding district. The entrance to the airfield and Technical Site was from the guardroom and all the traffic coming from the Domestic and Hospital Sites made for a very busy crossroads junction with the local traffic on the Half Mile Road going to and from Woodbridge town. As a result of this the RAF Police set up a road traffic control with the Police giving hand signals to enable the military traffic to cross in safety. There was some controversy as to whether the civilian traffic on the main road to Woodbridge should have to stop and give way, but it worked rather smoothly despite a little aggravation from time to time. The RAF Police were working very closely with the USAF Police, who would share in and eventually assume full responsibility for this traffic control.

The Americans found it strange that the public road ran so close to the airfield boundary and aircraft parking dispersals, particularly at Wood Barn Corner, with local traffic also intersecting with the HQ Site entrance. An application to the Highways Department would be made to investigate a possible re-routing of the public road between

Ivy Lodge and the Officers' Club, with a roundabout to overcome the junction of military and public traffic, but it was feared that any decision would be a long time coming.

Word came in that the 200 RAF personnel were soon to be pulling out. A bit of a shock that after only a few months they should be going but it seems that it was always on the cards after the Americans had learnt the ropes regarding the handling of security, the way in which to purchase items required by the military locally and the British laws enforced by the local constabulary. From the mid-1970s the local Tunstall policeman, PC Burman, had his own office at Bentwaters, adjacent to the USAF police admin block, so as to be on hand to deal with any problems relating to UK law.

Another important post would be that of a Public Relations officer, who would work very closely with the Wing Commander to assist the USAF cultivating good working relationships with their British hosts at every level. The very competent Miss Jackie Errington, who was highly respected by the USAF Commanders and their families, occupied this post from the mid-1960s.

The only RAF connection would be a RAF Squadron Leader 'Station Commander' who would be a Liaison Officer to co-ordinate between the RAF and the American Wing staff. In view of his important role he was allocated one of the first completed Married Quarters.

The RAF Station Commander also had a particular interest in the British Staff Organisation (BSO) responsible for the employment of all civil servants working alongside the Americans. Miss Mary Everest was № 2 in the BSO office when I first had the pleasure of meeting her. It was clear that with Mary's efficient office management she would soon become № 1 and would take charge of running things for many years – right up to the Base's closure in 1993.

Local traders were being contracted to sell some of the consumable items not yet available through the AFEES, like fresh fruit, etc. A local farmer was provided with a small building to set up what was to be known as a *Vegomart* that proved a very worthwhile move to benefit all concerned.

Another worthwhile scheme was the *Tea Shack*. There were now so many small civilian sub-contractors fitting out the various electrical and mechanical alarm systems and controls, not to mention the British Telecommunications workmen, all looking for refreshments, but they could not use the BX where everything was in dollar currency. The Tea Shack was on the grass verge approach to the main entrance to the airfield, adjacent to the main guardroom on private land (not government), to the relief of all those who did not have dollars to spend and were now able to enjoy their cuppa. This shack would only be allowed to stay in that location for a short while, however, since it was not in keeping with what the base authorities were trying to achieve. Most civilian staff would bring their own refreshments with them. The AMWD employed a tea boy.

Recruitment of civilian firemen was ongoing to man the small fire station adjacent the main guardroom. A second fire station adjacent the control tower was manned by military personnel, operating shiftwork around the clock to cover flying activities.

91st Squadron, with their F86 Sabre jet aircraft, were settling in with four aircraft standing on the readiness pad on the edge of the 26-08 runway at all times.

The motor vehicle traffic and others wishing to cross the main runway using the taxiway would cross on a green traffic light at the 26 ends only. This practice would be changed as soon as possible at the request of the Air Traffic Controller with all future traffic crossing the old and disused 32-14 runways. This brought the vehicle traffic nearer to the tower for better control. With all the 91st Squadron activities, munitions areas, aircraft

maintenance (to name but a few) having their workforce on the other side of the airfield, there would be scores of runway crossings every day.

The delays in waiting to cross the runway, not to mention the dangers of doing so, would be covered in a later chapter.

Let us now meet some of the USAF airmen who were at Bentwaters in 1951....

Mason Hier was a young airman based at Burtonwood (near Warrington in Cheshire) in the late 1940s. Burtonwood had been a supply base during WW2 for the US Army Air Force wartime bases. Mason was instructed to deliver what he called a '6-wheeler' to Bentwaters from Burtonwood as soon as

RAF Standard Vanguard pickup.

possible; quite a trip of well over 200 miles with very few dual carriageways in the 1950s. Mason returned to Burtonwood the next day, not knowing that his next stay at Bentwaters would be for a three-year stretch. It must be mentioned that very early after the Americans arrived, a fleet of British Standard Vanguard pickup trucks was delivered to Bentwaters. The RAF were already using this type of runaround vehicle and could have advised the USAF to go for a fleet of these as a stopgap until their own vehicles arrived from the States but it has to be admitted that the linkage to change the gears that was mounted on the steering column of the Vanguard was not the best and with such a high number of these vehicles in dock for mechanical faults, the Americans were not impressed.

This is what Howard Meyers, a new arrival at the base remembers about the early days at Bentwaters. He writes:

The 91st, 92nd and 116th (Washington Air Guard) were the first to arrive during the Korean War after flying their F86s over via Newfoundland, Iceland, Scotland and finally to Bentwaters. Both the airdromes had been idle since WWII and, needless to say, it took much elbow grease to become operational. The group was headed by a very capable cadre of commanders (ie: Colonel Pinkston, Colonel Carrigan, Colonel Cassidy and Squadron Commanders Colonel Carlyle and Colonel Frost.)

In the two years that I spent as a member of the group many friendships were cemented amongst the locals that are still in effect today; as a matter of fact, I married one of the locals. Hopefully this will clarify some of the history of the 81st Wing.

As we approached Christmas 1951 we were seeing an increase in the volume of traffic on our narrow country roads and there had already been some minor accidents involving US airmen who had chosen to ship their large Studebaker and Cadillac cars across the Atlantic. Police Constable New of Eyke police station was forever missing his meal break to attend to minor accidents. The 'motor pool', as it was known, developed a driving school to help alleviate the traffic problems that were now a matter of urgent attention as new airmen were introduced to driving 'on the wrong side of the road'.

Mr Leslie Dunnett, a retired police sergeant of the Suffolk constabulary, was employed to help run this driving school, which was a 'must attend' for all new arrivals.

Leslie Dunnett was the first of nine retired police constables to be employed at the base in the early days of its development, which was a good move on the part of the RAF civilian employers office to give all the new airmen some useful tips on the dos and don'ts of behaviour during their stay here.

Leslie's job was eventually taken over by the late Bill Felgate, who saw the driving school extend into the 1980s and 90s, proving to be a very worthwhile facility.

We were now getting to know the mess hall personnel, especially Chuck Wrobel and Sergeant Jake, the chief cook, with full responsibility to get the food online in time. Chuck was a young 18-year-old put into the kitchen to cook and generally wash the odd pot and pan throughout that long night shift.

We had our laughs. I remember the ministry electrician Arthur Parker or 'Heff', as we called him, was a member of the Salvation Army and keen to sell as many copies of their publication *War Cry* as he could. Sergeant Jake ran up a bill for many weeks supply of the War Cry but when approached by Heff, who reminded him that he owed 1s 6d for the three months' worth of papers, Jake replied, "Gee Heff, that's a beer and a half!"

Heff became the airfield electrician, which was now a full-time job, assisted by Brian and Cyril. The new airfield lighting system was in demand and throughout the winter period in particular there was never a slack period.

Winter Flying – 1952

Experiencing our first winter with the USAF as our guests, we wondered how 'the troops', as we called our workforce, would respond, as they had to fulfil their operational requirements. One of the most important tasks was to keep the runways and taxiways clear of snow. It must be said that the USAF were well prepared with all the proper equipment to meet adverse weather conditions.

The problem with some of the heavy snow moving equipment was that the airfield lighting would get broken as the scraper blades shaved the tarmac and concrete surfaces. Replacement of damaged light fittings was a continuous job for Heff and his men throughout the winter months.

Payment for items that were issued as spares was arranged through the stores with copies of all pay statements going to the BCE. This would turn out to be a very large accounting job that would entail many staff, for which the BCE would be happy to employ British civil servants who would become familiar with both US and British currency.

We had industrial action at Bentwaters when the aircraft fuel tanker drivers went on strike. All the tankers were marked Mobil Oil and deliver fuel to the storage tanks on a regular basis. This particular day they chose to walk out of the gate and leave their tankers standing behind the Liquid Oxygen plant adjacent the bulk fuel compound. Can you imagine the difficult situations that were likely to occur if the storage tanks run dry?

We had our American allies over here and were hoping that the strike could be resolved very soon, certainly before there was an alert calling for air action of any magnitude. Fortunately the dispute was quickly resolved but it was a warning of trouble that we could do without. The authorities would now have their eyes on this and would be planning a more reliable way to keep the tanks filled up.

The AMWD staff was now increasing to several dozen men and women and the payment of these in cash would also be an important undertaking. The Clerk of Works, Mr Arthur Morgan (who had been a prisoner of war in the Far East during World War II after the fall of Singapore) was responsible for collecting hundreds of pounds in cash from Barclays Bank in Woodbridge to correctly make up each wage packet for payday at lunchtime every Thursday, a very responsible part of his weekly work and a risk that he and the driver were prepared to take. I'm not sure if anyone would want to do so now.

We had a period when there was a good deal of overnight frost, which resulted in frozen pipes; not a happy time for those rising early to start the early shift. They would have to miss that clean shaven look and hope that the Squadron commander would understand the problem. The Commander himself was staying in a local hotel where things were no doubt a little more comfortable. Conditions on the base were somewhat bleak for the next few weeks.

Come lunchtime each day the outside temperature would have reached well above freezing point, when most folk would have the opportunity to clean up, only to await nightfall and experience another icy blast.

With clear blue skies during the daytime flying was always on going. The F86 Sabres would head out to the north up the coastline to designated areas for their training, perhaps on the odd occasion with the RAF Meteors.

These training exercises were a great advantage to both sides, especially as the F86 could reach Mach 1, which is when the aircraft goes through the sound barrier. As well as being an extremely good fighter aircraft in my view the F 86 Sabre looked good as well.

With springtime approaching the airfield grass areas were greening up and the grass cutting was arranged to be carried out by a landscape contractor. It was a full time job with hundreds of acres of grass to keep under control.

Everyone had been made aware that Foreign Object Damage was a serious issue and that the runway surfaces must be kept clear at all times. Another important consideration was the risk of 'bird strike' which needed to be dealt with by issuing a separate contract to those trained in the business of bird deterrent and control.

The airfield ground staff responsible for ground signals and aircraft marshalling were equipped with a bird scarer that they could deploy as they speed up and down the runway. It emitted a loud screaming noise to clear the area of all birds just before the aircraft take off.

A trained Falconer widow sparrowhawk or similar bird of prey would also be supplied by a specialist contractor to patrol the airfield boundary and any areas where small birds might flock together in order to keep them clear of aircraft taxiway areas and runways.

We became aware that the birds were attracted to short cut grass and so we had to work out areas most important to flying and in particular areas where jet aircraft were likely to taxi in preparation for take off. Instructions were given to leave grass in these areas to grow to 12 ins or more each side of the runway and extending out from the runway edge 20 yards or more to deter birds from that area of the airfield.

It made the airfield look untidy when compared to the early days of RAF Stations and the Spitfire era when the Station Commander would expect his airfield to look spick and span in every respect, especially for the dreaded annual AOC's inspection. But jet engines were so powerful that they would suck in foreign objects and small birds like a vacuum cleaner if there were any in the vicinity and if leaving the grass to grow long helped to alleviate this danger then it was a small price to pay.

81 Wing had been at Bentwaters for almost a year now but there was still such a lot that needed to be done. Each squadron had submitted a list of requirements and it was going to be a difficult job to decide on an order of priority that would please everyone.

The BCE squadron drawing office would need to make drawings of each squadron's new facilities, as requested, and get their Squadron leader to check that it was exactly what they wanted before the drawings were presented to the approval committee.

The BCE would pass to the AMWD any projects that had been funded in the order of priority that they were to be constructed.

There were already two projects ongoing to be completed in the mid-1950s – a new Fire Station on the north of the airfield and a workshop complex to the west of Hangar 74 on the south east of the airfield.

As I said earlier, the rebuilding of Bentwaters was a major undertaking and would take 40 years and many million of bucks.

The Cold War was ongoing and 81st Fighter Wing would rise to the challenge provided they had the right facilities to do the job. My intention is to record the development of the base year-by-year over the next 40 years, to give some idea how the US Air Force grasped the nettle and got on with it.

Two-ship F-86 Sabre lift-off from the Bentwaters runway. [USAF]

The electrical supply line from the National Grid being totally inadequate to handle the power required to serve a Grade A NATO Operational Military Base, a new underground cable was laid for many miles to the nearest substation, connecting it to the Base's substation with new switchgear included. The existing AMWD standby generator and (the same one our Mr Hicks worked on the night the FIDO was lighting our skies) would also be upgraded.

The water supply and storage would not be sufficient to meet demand and as the base needed to support itself for this service, an additional high-level tank would be erected beside the existing tank adjacent the old NAAFI. This meant that a team of civil engineers would inspect the disused high level water storage tanks on the now disused World War 2 American bases to organise the relocation of a suitable additional second tank for Bentwaters. A suitable replacement tank was eventually found at the former US Air Force base at Boxted in Essex.

The water borehole pump that had supplied the water from 70 feet down for the RAF in the early days would also be replaced with a larger pump to a deeper level to meet the increase in demand.

Water supply to the far side of the airfield was to be undertaken on a major scale since the only existing supply in that area was for fire hydrants.

The Half Mile Road is overgrown and has been unused for many years but we should remember that until the year 1961 it was the main road to and from Woodbridge town. Lottie and I would catch the Eastern Counties bus at the top of the road outside the Guardroom to go to the shops in Woodbridge and even the flicks in the evening.

While we are on the subject of water it should be mentioned that in the late 1940s after the war the local council raised a contract to connect a water distribution system providing the village of Tunstall with running water and also fire hydrant protection. A high level water tower was erected adjacent to Red House Farm just outside the RAF Bentwaters boundary.

Water mains were laid in the public road, connecting to the base water main for supply to the base should our borehole pump fail at any time, although due to our heavy demand for water the Water Company was never able to supply us, so the connection was never used. Proceeding to the entrance to the Officers club the contractor turned right to excavate in the old road, past the entrance to the HQ Site and skirting the edge of the airfield, past the guardroom and down the Half Mile road to Tunstall. It is still, as far as I know, the main supply of water to Tunstall, despite the changes and the new road layout.

A major survey was ongoing to get main sewer drainage to the airfield side of the Half Mile Road and this was one of the top priorities on the Commander's list, the 'honey bucket' situation being to nobody's liking. If undertaken the sewage pipes would have to cross this busy road to get the effluent pumped to the base sewage works located near Rendlesham Hall. You may ask what the sewage works for Bentwaters were doing at Rendlesham Hall. The answer is that since there was already a sewage works there, which had been for many years serving the hall and had excess capacity, the MOD decided that it would be sufficient for the requirements of what they believed at the time would be only a temporary wartime base.

It goes without saying that the sewage works would need to be upgraded and enlarged to deal with the increased volume of greatly enlarged base.

By the mid-1952 the number of US Air Force personnel and their dependents arriving called for a school to be set up to deal with the large number of children requiring educational facilities. Since these children were so scattered in their village rented homes, arrangements would need to be made to bus them to Bentwaters morning and afternoon. A contract with the local bus company was

established and for those children who lived in remote locations a special bus service was established to collect them individually.

It should be pointed out that some of the service families were living more than 30 miles from the base in places such as Stowmarket, Wableswick, Framlingham and Southwold, to name but a few. The schooling for the Bentwaters children would be a bone of contention for many years to come.

The school was established in the wooden and tin huts that had previously been the troops shower rooms, along with any other spare buildings dotted around the base that were considered suitable for the teachers to take classes.

The school Principal had a difficult job to administer school under such conditions, not to mention staff problems, a playground area that was continually flooded with rainwater and a cleaning contractor who found it difficult to find enough staff.

Mr Souders was the Principal and from what I knew of him he was an ideal man for the job. He had a military appearance about him, very upright and always one of the smartest dressed men on Bentwaters. Sadly he died soon after retirement but I had the pleasure of speaking to his daughter Judith in the early part of 2003 and she said that my description of him was correct. She said that she and her brother had fond memories of their local English schooldays in Suffolk. The Souders family lived in Woodbridge Town in one of the big houses that looked down Warren Hill Road. Her brother gained a scholarship and was a very proud student at the local college. Judith said she was only 4 years old when they arrived in the UK and over 50 years later is still living in Norwich. She loves it and hopes her child would grow up to enjoy a world that is free from the Cold War or anything resembling it.

I remember that Mr Souders left Bentwaters school to work in Germany for a year or two and on his return to the Twin bases took over the Woodbridge school with an office staff of three or four. One of them was an American lady called Juanita, who was Deputy Head at Woodbridge Elementary School and who has stayed to live in Woodbridge Town on retirement and who again I'm sure will be enjoying the quiet life.

Another very important part of the American serviceman's life was his automobile and the fuel to get it around. As I have mentioned some of the personnel shipped their large Ford, Chrysler or Cadillac cars over here to provide personal and family transport, which was essential if the accommodation they were renting was way out in the sticks.

Needless to say, the other important consideration was the Airman himself and getting to and from work but the Americans were soon to discover that their large gas

guzzling cars were very expensive to run at British fuel prices which were nearly 4 times those in the USA. This resulted in another important project between the Air Force and the (BX) Base Exchange to provide the necessary funds to construct a petrol and vehicle service station as soon as possible.

One of the many services that the (BX) provided was automatic vending machines that delivered candy bars, cigarettes and drinks, etc at the push of a button. These machines were located in the corner of workshops, aircraft hangars and any other suitable buildings with a power supply. However these American-made machines required a 110 volt supply whereas the British electricity supplies 240 volts. This gave the electrical contractors plenty to do in wiring new power circuits. Some of the vending

Mechanics working on an F-86 Sabre, Bentwaters 1952. [USAF]

Nissen hut containing Woodbridge Dining Hall on a grey and misty day in the fifties. [RH]

Tin Huts become temporary school buildings with the arrival of new barrack blocks for the airmen. [USAF]

machines were fitted with a transformer to overcome the voltage difference where 110 volt wiring did not exist.

Since these vending machines accepted US coins only, the British guys working on the base were in a situation that if they did not remember to bring enough cigarettes with them in the morning to last the day they would need to go to the Tea Shack by the guardroom or head to the village shop.

There was no way that the Airmen could help them because the exchange of Lucky Strike or Camel cigarettes for money or any merchandise was totally prohibited and it was common for those leaving the base to be searched by the resident Customs Officer. As one left the job at the end of the working day approaching the main exit gate the officer would ask to search your lunch box for any

items that were subject to tax duty. They did have some success in this regard but with risk of losing your job very few were prepared to get involved.

One enterprising member of our team brought a few packets of English cigarettes to work with him in a case to sell to his workmates if they had run out, which helped us get over the problem. I wasn't sure if there was anything illegal about this but as far as I know he never got into any trouble.

The contract for the construction of the new Chapel went to Cubit and Gotts, the contractor that was already doing the day-to-day maintenance. It was to be situated on the road junction that led to the airmen's billets.

The new Library was located on the same junction, on the opposite side of the road adjacent to the water tower. Both contracts were to be completed in 1953. Both buildings were retained in the new housing development at Rendlesham Park in 2004.

Mr George Ward was the site foreman for the chapel, a very hard working man, I remember, and never afraid to join in and help the men to get it done.

The base Fire Station, which was located adjacent the guardroom, was proving inadequate. There had been a recruitment drive to employ civilian firemen to assist with the round-the-clock cover necessary, but accommodation was non-existent for 24-hour shift work, with the firemen using billets as

rest rooms. A new station was listed as a top priority.

In this year 1952 the pressure to get well and truly stuck-in and rebuild Bentwaters was being highlighted by every Squadron and more and more money was forthcoming to fund the urgent projects.

The Air Ministry Works Department was to set up a Part One Section that would handle all government management of the new construction work. The staff would include a Resident Engineer, who was to be assisted by senior and junior Clerk of Works who would be the contact for the building contractor.

F-86 Sabre in clear skies over East Anglia – 1950s.

Visitors queue to take a look inside the cockpit of an F-86 Sabre on Bentwaters Open Day 1953.

The Duke of Edinburgh is the first VIP to visit the USAF at Bentwaters in 1953. [EADT]

Colonel Carrigan gives the Duke a guided tour of the F-86 Sabre. [USAF]

The Rebuild Begins – 1953

The new Resident Engineer was Mr Ron Stewart, a very keen young engineer eager to see that his staff took their responsibilities seriously and who expected a first class job from the contractor and a first class finished building that met all aspects of the specification.

One incident comes to mind that Ron would have remembered. It was in the early days of letting contracts at RAF Woodbridge and this particular contractor received a delivery of bricks that were 'loose loaded' onto the truck, which means that each individual brick had been thrown onto the truck and not stacked in neat packs, as one would expect.

The contractor made another mistake when he told the truck driver to tip them up onto the concrete surface for the brick layers to sort and lay. Ron Stewart did not hesitate to go over to the contractor and condemn the entire load of bricks, instructing him to remove them from the station. It goes without saying that the bricks were so damaged that they were suitable only for placing in a floor area as a sub base for concreting over.

Such would be the way the AMWD supervisors would deal with any contractor who thought that anything would do.

Everyone involved became more observant, particularly the Foremen of Trades (FoT), who monitored the contract work throughout the day, even extra time spent on site while the contractor was working.

Every week the workload of the Part One team under Ron Stewart increased and their number rose from 12 to 14. These craftsmen all had contract work experience in different building trades to give the RE full cover of each trade supervised on his behalf.

We had at that time under construction a Chapel, Library, New Fire Station, Rod and Gun Club, Top Four Club and Hangar building number 74 annex workshops.

The RE was working closely with Captain Bill Jeans, who was assisting the BCE to the point that they met almost every day to confer and confirm that the Base Commander, to whom the BCE was answerable, was happy with progress and quality of work and being on target to meet completion dates. The BCE was at present holding the rank of Major but that was expected to change because the amount of projects involved called for him to be upgraded to Lt Colonel.

The need for permanent Married Quarters was recognised and a design team put to work to establish the siting and the type of structure they would take.

Events under consideration were an Armed Forces Day and a VIP visit.

1953 had hardly begun when the East Coast experienced the most severe floods it has had to withstand for almost 100 years. Areas flooded included Langer Road and the RAF Sea Plane Base at Felixstowe. Most of the families in this area had to be evacuated.

All electric power failed and most of the furniture and personal belongings were lost. Arthur Parker (Heff), our airfield electrician and his family were among the unfortunate families to be flooded out of their homes in

Langer Road, which was very stressful at the time. The same situation existed at Orford and all low-lying areas along the coast at Aldeburgh, Thorpeness, Wableswick, Southwold and further north to Lowestoft and the entire Norfolk coastline.

The reason I mention this never forgotten winter storm is the effect it had on the Bentwaters personnel. I had spoken about the American service personnel living in some of the most outlandish places and these were the people who would find it very difficult to make the base for duty and sort out their flooded homes. Everyone threw their weight behind the clearing up operation and it has to be said the American airmen were very gallant in some of the rescues that they made. Some returned 50 years later to enjoy a reunion with the British families and appeared on TV as a reminder of those dreadful times. The Base personnel and the military offered a lot of help to the local people with teams of airmen clearing public areas and providing food and blankets for the old and infirm.

I must mention one airman with whom I was acquainted who lived in Wableswick had recently bought himself a second-hand British car that was never going to be a classic or give him good service, so he helped it over the edge and enjoyed the replacement vehicle that the insurance company provided.

The Armed Forces Day was an occasion that we in this country would call an Open Day and was to be held in the early spring of 1953. These special days were usually on a Saturday and afforded an opportunity for Air Force personnel to show their families their place of work and for the first time the British Public were invited in to view the aircraft. The Air Force personnel played Baseball at the Ivy Lodge gate location, an area suitable for their national game.

Entrance was free to all with free parking for everyone to enjoy a day out with the US Air Force. Local Suffolk residents would be especially welcomed and given the opportunity to get a closer look at the aircraft

that were now a part of their daily lives and to chat to their American neighbours about their stay in Suffolk – and, of course, the weather!

My family enjoyed the day along with our friends, who were surprised by the close proximity of the aircraft as they taxied by in full view through our kitchen window, since we were so close to the main aircraft taxiway. Aircraft had flown in from other bases to visit Bentwaters for the day and were lined up on the runway. Steps were provided to allow anyone interested to get a close look inside the cockpit. I remember that it was not a particularly warm day. Airfields are never warm, even at the best of times, given that they are open to the elements, but on this particular day the wind was blowing from the northeast and Bentwaters was particularly cold when the wind blew from that direction.

The large transport aircraft in particular were impressive to the local people, many of whom declared it a miracle that they managed to get airborne. The public always liked to step into these monsters so Dick Woods and Ted Smart, two carpenters employed directly by the BCE, constructed a ramp to the nose entrance of a Globemaster for everyone to enjoy the feeling of being inside this cavernous aircraft.

The RAF would always attend these shows and put on an air display as well as static displays featuring various aircraft with information boards giving performance details etc. I remember M/Sgt Wolf, the Chief of BCE instructing young airmen to put these info boards in front of particular aircraft, although even he got a little puzzled between his Chipmunk and his Tiger Moth.

That first Bentwaters Open Day there were grey skies but it was an enjoyable day all the same. The flypast aircraft in those days were Spitfires, Hurricanes, Dakotas and Lancasters, all propeller aircraft of World War II vintage. In comparison the USAF Sabre jets were a novelty and grabbed the attention of the spectators, leaving them in no doubt that these were the aircraft of the future.

The USAF, we soon found out, was one of the best Air Forces at generating rubbish. In all the low lying areas there were places that we called 'pits' where, many years ago, the local inhabitants had excavated sand or gravel for use in making mortar for building work or to surface bridleways, later to become roadways. Where there was clay suitable for making bricks or tiles a kiln would be built to supply these building materials to the local area. Where this material had been removed there would be deep depressions and over the years these had been left to become overgrown.

In some instances the bottom of the pit could be 20ft below the surrounding area, giving a good start to dig further down to reach the water table. Anywhere that cottages had been constructed it was essential to dig a well to provide drinking water and this well was often situated at the bottom of the pit.

Now what has all this to do with the USAF at Bentwaters? Such a water well had existed at Bentwaters Cottage, not far from the church that stood just outside the airfield boundary. The cottage had been demolished in the late 1940s and the brick rubble from the demolition was dumped into the pit. So we had a situation where the dumping of rubbish had been started in the 40s and there was every opportunity to continue tipping the rubbish from the Base into the pit until it was levelled over with soil to make a nice area for the American lads to play basketball. The well would not see daylight again.

Another important event for the 81st Wing to look forward to was the visit by the Duke of Edinburgh on May 22nd 1953, when he was welcomed by Colonel Bob Garrigan and invited to meet the American aircrews now flying over Suffolk at the speed of sound.

The RAF aircrews would receive the supersonic Hawker Hunter in 1953. British pilot Neville Duke had been test flying this aircraft and attempting to break the airspeed record over a given area of the English Channel. Of course that great American aviator Chuck Yeager (an ex WWII fighter pilot ace who had been based at Leiston in Suffolk during the war) had become the first to reach the speed of sound in a small jet aircraft called a Bell in 1947.

But the tiny Bell aircraft had no practical applications, having been specifically designed to break the sound barrier. In order to do so it was carried in the bomb rack of a Stratofortress to a height of several thousand feet and released. Following that landmark the development of jet aircraft proceeded at an amazing pace and now, just a few years later, there were supersonic military aircraft in service. Neville Duke famously broke the sound barrier in a Hawker Hunter at the Farnborough Air Show in 1952. Below is an extract from one of the Base Newsletters, written by a US Airman bystander just after the Duke's visit.

81st FIGHTER INTERCEPTOR WING RAF STATION BENTWATERS May 1953

Flown by 32 of the best damn fighter jocks of the best damn Fighter Wing of the USAF. The occasion of this flyover was a visit to Bentwaters by the Duke of Edinburgh on May 22nd 1953. Sixteen F-86s from the 91st FIS were scrambled then joined by sixteen 92nd FIS F-86"s from Shepherds Grove for a 400mph pass at 500 feet. Three F86s – two from the 91st and one from the 92nd – created a sonic boom from 40,000 feet just as the last of the massed flight cleared the fence.

Pilots from the 91st Sqdn. were: Barrett, Courtney, Butterfield, Krisle, Hagarty, Barnes, Eckman, VaMatre, Williams, Hoye, Herring, Perkins, Myers, Stabley, Gathercoal, and Fortney.

From the 92nd Sqdn. were: Owens, Ashcraft, Davenport, Doty, Fluitt, Leidy, Marsh,

Creating the sonic boom were Pytel and Kirk from the 91st and Pile from the 92nd leading the scramble and fly-by was Major Sandy Moats. Sandy was based with 323FG at Bodney in Norfolk and Fowlmere in Cambridgeshire during WW2 as a Mustang P51 fighter pilot. By the time Sandy had completed his service career he reached the rank of a Three Star General.

Bentwaters was to have a major runway extension programme and other facility upgrades to meet Strategic Air Command (SAC) requirements and enable the landing and take-off of other types of aircraft that may need to use the Bentwaters runway. While this work was in progress the F-86A aircraft would be relocated to the continent, where they would carry on their operational training. The control tower would be prepared for a roof top cabin with all the radio and communications wiring that was involved.

The Base Civil Engineer would get the opportunity to design an aircraft braking system known as an *arrestor barrier* – similar to the earlier type fitted on aircraft carriers. With the runway to be extended an opportunity also arose to connect the underground services such as water pipes and electric power supply cables to the south side

Major Sandy Moats (centre) led the F86 flypast. He is flanked by pilots Lt Pytel and Lt Kirk. [EADT]

of the airfield and to the hangars, building 74 and workshops.

Completion of the new four-bay fire station was expected soon and hopefully with fine weather in the summer and autumn every project would meet its completion date.

The contract for the first Married Quarters was about to be let to a contractor named Ames from Lowestoft who were to build 40 single-storey two and three bedroom units at Bentwaters and 240 units at RAF Sutton Heath, about 10 miles from Bentwaters.

Sutton Heath was another base which the USAF had taken over and based the 79th Squadron operating Thunderjets under the command of the 20th TFW with its HQ at Upper Heyford. Sutton Heath, which would be renamed Woodbridge, was well known during WW2 for its FIDO system that enabled damaged aircraft to land in foggy conditions, saving aircraft and aircrew.

The old tin huts on Site 4 at Bentwaters that were converted to married quarters in the days of the RAF would not be used by the Americans for the same purpose; instead they would be used by single officers, pilots, etc, with a cleaning contractor in attendance. This arrangement was not without its comments. Site 4 would become known as 'Sin City' although it was never explained why! Three two-storey blocks were to be constructed adjacent the officers mess to accommodate visiting officers and these would also have a contract cleaning arrangement.

No married quarters were built at Wartime RAF Sutton Heath. The new bungalows were prefabricated and would become known as *tobacco bungalows* as the cost to erect them would be paid by the British Government in return for money owed to the US for tobacco imports. The new Tobacco Bungalows would be erected each side of what had been the 'carriage drive' used by Lord Rendlesham's horse and carriage between Eyke Lodge (known to some as 'The Italian Lodge') and Rendlesham Hall.

The carriage drive was lined with trees each side, mainly oak and lime trees, to enhance the drive for his Lordship's pleasure. Sadly these had to be removed and the main contractor let this work out to a subcontractor, Mr Arthur Clarke, who had named his company 'Blast That Stump'. Very appropriate!

Ron Stewart would oversee this as one of his major projects, were now totalling well over a dozen ongoing on both the Bases. The cost of these projects would total over £2 million (and we are talking about 1953 prices[1]). The supervisory staff to assist the RE to oversee these projects would increase to 18 Clerks of Works and Foremen of Trades.

Mr Jock Dunnet would oversee the Bentwaters Married Quarters Project, now progressing as fast as possible to allow the important operational officers to live on base to manage urgent military business.

A large number of fir trees needed to be removed to get the Woodbridge Married Quarters up and running this work was carried out by the Forestry Commission. The lumber would go to the mining region to serve as pit props. Another contract was soon issued to construct new Barrack Blocks to replace the Nissen huts that previously served as the airmen's billets. The six new Barrack Blocks would be two-storey brick construction with a centre corridor that would become a bone of contention in time to come.

Preparations were ongoing for a change of command. The new wing commander was to be Colonel Harold Holt and the new Base Civil Engineer to be Major Maney. The role of BCE would turn out to be a tough assignment through the period 1954/55 with the ongoing construction of such a large number of major new projects.

A change of the type of aircraft to be based at Bentwaters was to take place during 1954 from the F86 Sabre to the F84 Thunderstreak;

Woodbridge control tower with top cabin. [LB]

this would also mean the wing operational status would be changed from 81st Fighter Wing to 81st Fighter Bomber Wing.

The Thunderstreak is very similar to the Thunderjet, which is based at nearby Sutton Heath with the 79th Squadron under the command of the 20th Fighter Bomber Wing at Upper Heyford. The Thunderjet is a square wing aircraft whereby the Thunderstreak is swept wing.

The F84 is a heavier aircraft and when fully laden would be rocket assisted during takeoff. The weight of the F84, even unladen, would be something of a problem with its high landing speed; this aircraft had no drag chute to assist the pilot in emergency braking.

It was nevertheless an aircraft brought "to strengthen NATO for the benefit of the Western European Nations and to keep the Russians on their toes." This statement, made by a USAF General as he launched the new aircraft to be operated by the 81st Fighter

---

[1] Adjusted for inflation, £2 million in 1953 would equate to about £18 million in 2016 (Editor).

Woodbridge main gate. [LB]

Bomber Wing, upset Russian Premier Nikita Khrushchev, who took exception to the number of American bases in the UK, stating that Britain had become "an aircraft carrier". Anglo-Russian relations had reached an all-time low in the 1950s.

As spring 1954 approached the strengthening and extension of the main runway was being completed. The new extension took the 26-08 runway to almost 9000 feet, which proved sufficient in due course for the faster and heavier aircraft that would later operate from this Class 'A' airfield.

During the over-slabbing and extending of the runway, a special arrestor barrier was installed at each end of the 26-08 runway. The installation and testing was carried out by the BCE airmen under the supervision of Major William Maney, the Officer in charge of Base Civil Engineering. The barrier project turned out to be a very trying time for all those involved. A very good account of the way things went is explained by Mr Derrick Booth, who was attached to the BCE, who writes:

Bentwaters was closed to flying in the late fall of 1953 after the old F-86s were flown out to France. Over the winter the main 08-26 runway was lengthened to almost 10,000 feet and overslabbed (strengthened), with a further 1,000 feet of compacted gravel overshoot added to each end. The increased runway length was dictated by the higher landing speed of the F-84F, and it was almost the maximum landing area that could be accommodated within the property held under the ownership of the Ministry of Defence.

As a further precaution against problems with higher landing speeds, the 81st Air Base Group civil engineer's office installed the strange, German-built MA-1A runway barrier on the southwest end of the 26 runway. In addition, it built a concrete access road and turnaround with a permanent operational pad for the mobile GCA trailer and coupled generator trailer. This replaced pierced steel planking (PSP) pad originally laid when the base was re-activated in 1951.

The first F-84Fs began to arrive in the spring of 1954 and were objects of curiosity to many of the personnel on the base. British civilians were also drawn to Bentwaters, hoping to catch a glimpse of the new aircraft as they landed close to the road at the Iken end of the runway. The old F-86s bodies had been polished aluminium and not painted except for squadron markings, but the new F-84F was painted in two-colour earth tones as a camouflage, similar to that of Royal Air Force aircraft in World War Two.

The early days after arrival were consumed with trial loading and unloading of external stores, fitting glass fibre drop tanks to extend range and, in the far recesses of the base in the woods to the east, there were trial loadings of nuclear tactical weapons, delivered mostly at night in C-120 transports. These weapons were stored in newly-constructed and hardened structures.

The increased take-off loading with additional fuel and heavy stores tested to the limit the power of the F-84F's single Wright J-65 engine. To increase the margin of safety, pilots of the 91st and 92nd began practicing with assisted take off (ATO) rockets attached to disposable mounting brackets near the rear of the fuselage but the abundant foul-smelling smoke emitted by the Teledyne rockets pervaded the tech site and led to complaints from ground staff such as firemen and outdoor aircraft maintenance workers, and from workers in offices near the flight line.

In the early summer of 1954 the pilot of an F-84F attempted to abort a take-off and called the tower for the protection of the runway barrier. Although the barrier was deployed, the aircraft failed to engage it properly and came to rest with the pilot unhurt off the end of the soft overrun at the end of runway 26. The aircraft was extensively damaged – and the unarmed nuclear weapon it was carrying was also damaged.

Colonel Harold Holt, the new, forceful, cigar-eating and feared commander of the 81st called for a full post mortem of the accident, and to the Fire Marshall, Major William (Meanie) Maney, commander of the Base Civil Engineer squadron, he demanded, "Why doesn't your goddamn rabbit catcher work?" He was referring to the MA-1A runway barrier and he made it clear that heads would roll if it was found to be one of his boys who had lost the first brand-new F-84F on active service through negligence.

To test the effectiveness of the runway barrier, an ageing open-cab General Motors Air Force 6x6 truck № USAF 4689881 was requisitioned from the motor pool and modified. The wheels and struts of the crashed F-84F were salvaged and bolted on fabricated steel false-work rigged to the front of the truck to replicate the aircraft and the truck bed was filled with PSP to weigh 20,000 pounds, the weight of a loaded F-84F at take-off. To give more authenticity, the front underbelly shape of the F-84F was fashioned from sheet metal. Extra wheels were added to the front pair of the original truck to improve the load carrying (albeit at the expense of steering control).

The daring plan was to have the as-yet unknown 'pilot' of the contraption – which became known as The Thing – begin his roll down runway 26 from the northeast threshold and go through the gearbox to achieve maximum speed as soon as possible. At that point the pilot would shift to neutral and fire the four ATO rockets attached to the rear. It was hoped the vehicle would then reach realistic speeds of an aircraft aborting take-off, say 120mph.

ATO rockets burned for about 45 seconds and much planning was done to decide where The Thing would reach maximum engine-driven speed and where the thrust from the rockets would drive the vehicle to the point of maximum speed just before it engaged with the runway barrier.

Then came the question of who would drive the lethal-looking contraption... Colonel Holt quickly and secretly decided that question. The next officer to be stopped by police off-base for speeding was his candidate, he told his Exec. He had to wait only a few days before a young 2nd Lieutenant was logged in a speed trap on the Woodbridge bypass.

"You have a choice," he told the young engineering officer. "You can suffer the fine from the civil court and detention from your commanding officer, or you can accept my punishment."

Not unsurprisingly, the officer chose Colonel Holt's option: to drive 'The Thing' as fast as he could!

Flying at Bentwaters was closed down on the first Saturday after finishing touches had been done to The Thing. Markers were set by the side of the runway to signify the last point where the driver must fire the ATO rockets. A crowd of interested watchers gathered on the southwest corner of Runway 26. Cameras were readied, then the signal to begin the roll was transmitted by Major Maney over the two-way radio. It seemed like a long time elapsed before the shape of The Thing appeared over infamous hill on the main runway and then, suddenly, there was a mighty bang as the ATO rockets fired.

The Thing crashed through the nylon webbing with its nose gear but failed to raise the steel cable that should have lodged high up the main struts before gathering the anchor chain behind it. The cable was designed to transfer the kinetic energy of the vehicle to the static mass of the anchor chain lying by the side of the runway until a total transfer had been made and no further forward motion of the vehicle was possible. The run was considered a failure.

Close examination after the test revealed several important points. First the driver rightly believed The Thing had failed to be properly arrested and he fired his reverse thrust ATO rockets in an attempt to stop the vehicle. The slow motion film showed the nylon webbing parted from the hold-down points before the steel cable was thrown high enough to engage the struts effectively.

Marks on the fairings of the salvaged undercarriage showed the cable marks of the original emergency were similar to those of Test Number One. A post mortem briefing with operators and riggers of the barrier revealed that in order to raise the nylon webbing as high as possible, the headline was over-tensioned and the shear pins connecting

it to the steel stanchions were deformed and they sheared at a much lower force than was called for in the design.

It should be remembered that no MA-IA barrier installed in the field had ever been caned for in-all emergency, so crews and fire departments throughout the United States Air Force that were flying F-84Fs were following the same reasoning as Bentwaters firemen. To make the contraption work, the nylon webbing just had to be tensioned up to keep the catenary curve in the head line as straight as possible. Right?

The following Saturday flying was again shut down at Bentwaters. Senior officials from 3rd Air Force HQ in Ruislip and Commanders from other squadrons flying F-84Fs, intrigued by stories and rumours from the first test run, gathered by the side of the runway. At the command to go, the driver of The Thing, emboldened now by his experience, cogged through his screaming gearbox and, on reaching the marker, fired his rocket engines, now increased from four to six. The noise of the bang from their firing came after a great cry went up from the watching crowd on both sides of the runway... "Here he comes!"

The nose gear of The Thing engaged the nylon webbing on this second run, stretched the webbing suspended between the stanchions, popped the press studs to free the steel cable and, throwing it high before the modified shear pins sheared away. The cable could be seen making a sinusoidal wave as it became airborne. The Thing engaged the barrier with a loud twang as the nylon stretched like a massive hunting bow and instantly there was an increasingly loud bell-like noise as hundreds of tons of 55lb anchor chain jumped around and absorbed the energy from the vehicle.

Before The Thing came safely to a stop on the overshoot of the runway, the anchor chain was all used up and it rose from the ground before coming to back to earth with a loud, clanking thud. Then there was only a silence until a great shouting and whooping broke out from the onlookers.

There were congratulations all around. The Thing was towed away in triumph before yielding to the cutting torches of obscurity the following week. It was rumoured it had reached 140mph, but there was no way of verifying that figure.

Thereafter all MA-IA barriers throughout the Air Force were modified and the standing operating procedures rewritten. Some months later an F-84F pilot, going very fast, hollered for the barrier from those on duty in the tower at Bentwaters. Up came the stanchions, released by solenoids controlled from the tower. Slam went the runaway F-84F. The cable engaged correctly and, to those looking through binoculars from the tower, it appeared that the plane had been snagged without calamity.

But what the watchers failed to notice was that all the anchor chain was used up and there was still forward motion on the aircraft. The last 100 feet of the chain on each side of the runway was airborne, as with the second test, but this time the heavy battleship chain whiplashed in the air and broke into several links and sections of chain. They were thrown many feet, some were never recovered. Fortunately, nobody was hurt by the flying debris, the pilot was unharmed and the aircraft was only superficially damaged.

Thanks Derrick.

The barrier testing was an important part of flying operations at Bentwaters through the 50s and would take its toll on some of the BCE Squadron staff, who had put in a lot of working hours to keep the barrier in working order.

So now at Bentwaters we had the 91st, 92nd and 78th Fighter Aircraft Squadrons, The Base Civil Engineering Squadron, The Transport and Police Squadrons and the Supply Squadron. Other squadrons that would be formed to support this very large operational NATO Wing were Mission Support Squadron, Moral, Welfare, Recreation and Services Squadron, Communications Squadron, Comptroller Squadron and Equipment Maintenance Squadron.[1]

Other facilities were being upgraded during the runway closure period: the Bulk Fuel Installations were extended to provide increased storage and the Weapons Area was made more secure.

The security police were now becoming dog handlers, a select few having been given training by the RAF Police in the handling of RAF-trained Alsatian Dogs. The dogs were on loan to the USAF Police to improve security and new dog kennels with special exercise areas had been constructed adjacent the weapons area.

1954 was a very busy year and Colonel Harold Holt, the 81st Wing Commander, was determined to turn this old WW2 base into a respectable NATO defence establishment that everyone could be proud of. One of the most important sections in this process of turning the base around was the Base Civil Engineering Squadron with its drafting section or *drawing office*, as we called it, making sure that projects submitted both for Sutton Heath and Bentwaters were presented with their proposals to Headquarters at Ruislip in such a manner that funding would be difficult to refuse. With many other USAF Fighter and Bomber bases elsewhere in the UK and Europe, there was always competition for the limited funding available.

Also at this time the 81st Equipment Maintenance Squadron was formed and would become the largest and most diverse aircraft maintenance squadron in the US Air Forces in Europe. It would earn eight Outstanding Unit Awards, two USAFE Unit

---

[1] For clarification, the word 'squadron' is used in the USAF where the RAF would use the word 'section'.

Maintenance Effectiveness Awards and the USAFE Daedalian Maintenance Award.

As we moved into 1955 the new aircraft were very, busy mainly out over the North Sea where the aircrews were now becoming familiar with areas like The Wash (the location used for bombing runs and target practice). The T33 two-seat trainer aircraft were getting a lot of flying hours in. There was always an influx of new pilots who needed to be familiarised with the airfield and its runway approaches, not to mention the Bentwaters flight pattern.

The new Chapel and Rod & Gun Club were about to come on stream, providing much needed recreation facilities, especially the Chapel with all the importance that it would have for many individuals.

The 40 new Married Quarters were making steady progress, with a completion date early the following year. In pairs they would be numbered 601A and 601B, etc although the bungalow that would be numbered 600 was late in completion as it was now decided to construct this quarter on an area that was separated from the line of the other 20 pairs, to accommodate the Wing Commander on the corner of the road intersection facing the new temporary bowling alley. Because Qtrs 600 was late in its completion, Qtrs 605A&B would be allocated to the Wing Commander and his family, giving them elbow room and a chance to entertain their squadron personnel.

The numbering of new buildings would prove difficult. To the BCE office it did not seem too complicated; as the newly-completed buildings were handed over to the military they were given the next number. The only problem with that was the Chapel was given number 523 and the Rod & Gun Club, way over on the airfield side, was given 524. Strange, but we would have to get used to it.

As I mentioned earlier, a new building was to be constructed adjacent the new tobacco bungalows – a four-lane Bowling Alley. The temporary Bowling Alley had been in one of the large metal Romney workshops on the Tech site, adjacent my cottage. I must say I was not sorry when it was moved adjacent to Qtrs 603. Quite a lot of noise comes from those skittles and bowling balls on impact.

Also in 1955, RAF Sutton Heath was renamed RAF Woodbridge.

The first of many Married Family Housing (MFH) units to be built at the Twin Bases.

Twin Bases Planned – 1950s

The bungalows on both bases were reaching completion stage. The 79th Fighter Bomber Squadron under the direction of the 20th TFW HQ at Upper Heyford had settled in at the newly-named RAF Woodbridge and were now taking up some of the Married Family Housing (MFH) bungalows and flying operational exercises over the skies of Suffolk. This would appear to have no connection with the activities at Bentwaters Base but all would be made clear as time goes on. The 79th squadron operated F84 Thunderjets These were very similar to the Thunderstreak but with square wings. The Thunderjets would no doubt have a different operational role to that of the Thunderstreak. A lot of work was to be done at RAF Woodbridge to prepare the base for operating jet aircraft – with the benefit of all the knowledge gained from what we had just experienced at Bentwaters.

Bentwaters families would take up some of the MFH at Woodbridge. The 81st Wing was gearing up to take over Woodbridge in a move that would eventually make Woodbridge and Bentwaters 'twin' bases. The Deputy or Vice Wing Commander for the 81st would get a double bungalow at Woodbridge, as would Colonel Ivan McElroy, the Wing Commander, who took up residence in the Quarters 606A&B at Bentwaters for his large family and entertainment needs.

I should break at this point to mention special operations that were going on at the time.

In the mid-1950s for a period of about four years Bentwaters was host to the 512th squadron of F-86Ds over from Manston. This night fighter version of the F86 Sabre Fighter had been operated by the 81st on the continent in training with the Meteor NF-11s.

These F86Ds had a pointed black nose which housed a radar dish, making it distinguishable from the F86 Sabre jet fighter. Sadly two F-86Ds were lost while training over the North Sea, which cast a shadow over the F-86Ds stay at the base.

The F86D or 'Dogs', as they were known, would be handed over to the Danish Air Force at a later date as the USAF took up the more advanced Convair F-102A night fighter.

In the autumn of 1955 the 79th Squadron of the 20th Fighter Bomber Wing began operating F-84F Thunderstreak, replacing the ageing Thunderjet. This was to be a two-year stopgap before another aircraft change was announced. A new Squadron Operations Block at Woodbridge was planned and scheduled for completion 1957/58.

The 40 married quarters at Bentwaters were now becoming occupied but the new service road that ran immediately in front of the quarters was soon underwater. The soakaways intended to deal with the rainwater were clearly inadequate. I was sent to investigate this new problem and remember being greeted by Mrs McElroy with the words: "Have you brought a boat? I cannot reach my car. The water is up to the top of the roadside kerb and we have to collect the schoolchildren."

The drainage system was soon upgraded to ensure that flooding did not recur.

Ames, the subcontractor for the heating and electrical work on these bungalows, was experiencing difficulties. The bungalows were fitted with a hot air heating unit with above-ceiling trunking to give immediate heat, as requested by the USAF. Unfortunately, the small pump on the heater unit would not draw fuel from the underground tank 200 yards away at the end of the row of married quarters. This proved so problematic that the contractor doubted whether this US-designed fuel supply would ever operate correctly. The director of the company said that he was so convinced that the design would not work that he was prepared to go to the States at his own expense to check out the pipe layout and prove a change was necessary. A variation order was given to the contractor to install a flow and return pipe system that travelled past each MFH. The fuel would be pumped under pressure by an Argosy pump, ensuring fuel supply to within 6 feet of each heat exchanger, which proved a satisfactory conclusion.

More problems were caused by the Bendix automatic washing machines in the kitchens. These were fixed to the floor by two expansion bolts to prevent the machine from dancing all over the place as it reached maximum spin. If the bolt was not set into the floor at full depth and well secured, the Bendix would find any weaknesses and the phone would soon start ringing. The BCE office was now operating a telephone hotline where any minor problems – electrical, plumbing or the like – could be reported by dialling 2929. This hotline was to be busy from the word go.

I must mention that lovely old Rendlesham Hall, standing just on the edge of the base boundary adjacent to Site 7 was demolished. Everyone thought this was a mistake, with the US Air Force in need of more office and storage space. After all, the British Army had used this charming building for a number of years and it would be ideal, if only as a temporary measure. Anyway, the salvage contractor would do nicely from all those lovely oak doors, panels and all the treasures such as roof lead and piping – all in short supply following the war.

This was followed by the demolition of High House at Campsea Ashe. As you will remember, this was my first place of work as pantry boy after leaving school. With his lordship and immediate family all now departed this world, Christopher, the great-grandson who inherited the title, was under pressure to find the dreaded Death Duties now due for payment to the government. One way to meet this huge expense was to sell off all the valuable items from the house, such as the oak and lead, etc, that would raise money to meet this very high payment. It was inevitable that the rest of the building would suffer as a consequence, so complete demolition was necessary. The Badminton Court and Stables would make ideal dwellings, as it proved in due course, with the Schreiber family taking over the remainder of the complex.

As with any workplace there was always the odd character that seemed to help the day along and the Twin Bases were no exception. There was Geoff Cook, remembered for his invention of the radio ferret; there was Station Engineer 'Smithy', the energetic type who loved a challenge, Butler, the fellow in charge of the stokers, who was rather lost or certainly appeared so, Dusty Durrant, the Woodbridge storekeeper, who had an answer for anything and would help anyone. We had Clerk of Works named Morgan who was not ready to forgive and forget his period as a prisoner-of-war in a Japanese camp during World War II and when he took afternoon tea with Hilda Toller it went on for hours. A few notable characters at to the Twin Bases who are remembered just for being themselves.

We must not forget the GI weddings. There had been many during WW2 and we were going to get more of them as time moved on. We had the 1953 wedding of Ron and Olive Harlan. They had been friends for the two years that Ron had been in this country and after marriage they lived in

Aerial views of the Twin Bases – Bentwaters (above) [EADT] and Woodbridge (below) [ST].

Walton, near Felixstowe, over the shop of Hall's Chemists. In 1955 Megan from Aldeburgh married Bob, here is what she says:

I was born and raised in Aldeburgh and, while still at school, started baby-sitting for American families who lived off-base in town. In July 1954 I became secretary at the 81st Medical Group (later 81st Tactical Hospital). The Hospital Commander at the time, and my first boss, was Major Glen A. Hoss. Captain Joseph Dillehay was Adjutant and M/Sergeant Leo Loughlin 1st Sergeant. What a different world I suddenly found myself in – but a small, friendly family who really took care of this almost 18 year old.

I married Sergeant Robert E. Winans in 1956, who was assigned to the hospital in 1955. We were transferred Stateside in 1958, to Stead AFB, just north of Reno, Nevada. I know my parents just knew that there were still cowboys and Indians chasing each other out in the Wild West. Reno was a total culture change from my home in Aldeburgh, England. Every single thing was different – the lifestyle, stores were open all the time, slot machines were in all the stores, the town did not turn off the lights, sleep was not on the menu. What a world!

Thanks Megan.

Megan was a typist who told me she had made a mistake on the typewriter one day and asked if anybody else in the office had a 'rubber' that she could use, not realising that in US terminology this did *not* mean an 'eraser' as it does in the UK.

"But the American lads would always laugh with you. They were such great guys," she says.

The year was now 1957 and – for the period 18th June to 8th July – Colonel Lester Krause Jnr was Wing Commander. Colonel Harry l. Crouch would take the Wing on 9th July for the next three years. Colonel Crouch would move into the newly constructed bungalow number 600 A&B, in an isolated corner of the housing site at the road junction with the BX site and

Site 7 (the airmen's billets). A new Wing Commander's four-bedroom bungalow was being designed and constructed on spare ground at the bottom of Site 5.

It was about this time that I had the pleasure of meeting Dennis Smith. Dennis was the BX Snack bar manager arriving from Woodbridge base to succeed the present manager, Mr Nunn (Nunny), who was approaching retirement. Nunny was one of the early BX staff to arrive at Bentwaters and was operating the Snack Bar Wagon as well as many other duties.

Our friendship extended to the construction of Dennis's own bungalow on the Aldeburgh Road at Knodishall, with which I gave him some help following the construction of my own self-help (DIY) bungalow at Friday Street Rendlesham. DIY was becoming popular. This was a great time in our working lives and we were proud of our achievements in building our own new accommodation after the years of austerity in the UK that had followed the war.

A number of the new Quarters were now occupied by various squadron commanders and officers who needed to be on the base to serve the Wing Commander in the event of emergency. There were practice alert exercises from time to time which involved the aircraft having to get airborne in a matter of minutes. The aircrews, of course, were in the Victor Alert hangar's Portakabins, sleeping on the job, as it were, ready for quick reaction and take off.

These practice exercises were sometimes costly, particularly where the contractor was denied access in certain buildings or areas. The contractor would submit day work sheets to claim for time lost where workmen were stopped for periods over 30 minutes. This would be an ongoing problem for years to come.

The Rod & Gun Club had been up and running as a leisure facility for the past few months. It had a coffee bar and the clay

The F86 D's operated from Bentwaters as Night Fighters, CW

This type of F-84 was operated by 79th Squadron at RAF Woodbridge, part of the 20th TFW Upper Heyford. [USAF]

A C123 Provider airlifted the 92nd Squadron equipment from RAF Manston to Bentwaters. [USAF]

pigeon traps were operating every day to offer recreation to all ranks for the benefit of those who were off duty.

Sadly, Major Maney, the Base Civil Engineer, who was living in the new Quarters 601B, had an accident that proved fatal while he was at the Gun Club. You will remember that Major Maney had been at the forefront of testing the MA1A aircraft arrestor barrier for the F-84.

A number of new facilities were coming into use and existing facilities were being extended. The old tin hut hospital complex was to get a new brick extension an operating theatre which would involve a great deal of upheaval for patients and air force staff. The workmen had to work in a very difficult environment. On one occasion in the new extension a plumber was getting his blowtorch warmed up when it threw a flame out into a room that at the time was full of fumes, which ignited to engulf the workman in a ball of fire. The plumber, Mr Hunt, was severely burnt and later died from his injuries.

Another facility being put to use was the enlarged Child Care Centre. With the new family housing now occupied, mothers were pleased to leave their offspring in care while they went to do their shopping off Base. The Base facilities could not offer a great deal of variety at this stage, since they had yet to extend the Commissary to provide a bigger choice of shopping for Air Force families.

The *Victor Alert Shelters* were up and in use. They were open-ended but did at least provide some protection against the weather.

A Tanker shop was now in place just beyond the new Rod & Gun Club and a Supply Office Block (Building 136) was constructed at the crossways with Ivy Lodge and the perimeter road – an urgently needed facility for the chief of Supply or 'Resources', as the US Air Force like to call them.

The American Army Air Force engineering team were on site to speed up the erection of *Butler sheds*, as they were called – an all-steel

type of workshop or warehouse. These would provide urgent shelter for the many ground crews and their equipment and would be erected onto the existing concrete dispersals.

While all this was going on the contractors were just completing the erection of eight similar type aircraft hangars along the edge of the old 32/14 runway to provide more shelter for aircraft and maintenance personnel.

Bentwaters was now looking a different airfield to what it had been a year or two ago. The Woodbridge runway was getting a resurface job, which meant that the 79th Squadron Thunderjets and Thunderstreaks were temporarily operating from Bentwaters. During this time a Thunderjet caught on fire in the process of running up the runway to take-off, which put the Bentwaters airfield out of action for a while. I don't know if the pilot was rescued or not.

There was difficulty in achieving the extension of the Bentwaters runway at the eastern end to achieve the desired 9,000+ feet due to the land beyond the boundary falling sharply down to a drainage culvert taking the surface water from the surrounding fields towards Butley Creek.

During no-flying periods, particularly weekends, this low area would be filled with hundreds of truckloads of special hoggin fill that was hauled all the way from Homersfield. To achieve the compaction of this fill in preparation for the runway extension large compaction rollers were on site. Eventually the new area was ready for the extension that would bring the runway to the desired length of 9000+ feet. Evidence of this can be seen to this day in how sharp the fall is down to the oiltrap that cleans the surface water before it discharges into the creek.

In 1958 Bentwaters would now accommodate the 92nd Squadron from RAF Manston. The 92nd had been at Manston for the past three years and the 81st Wing were now prepared to move them to Bentwaters to reduce the size of the Wing layout and no

An F-84F 'Thunderstreak' makes a rocket-assisted take-off at Bentwaters c.1955 (note that the Control Tower now has a top cabin). [HE]

doubt cut costs. The 92nd Squadron had moved to Manston in 1955 operating their F-84 Thunderstreaks. In 1956 eight of the 92nd Squadron aircraft took part in a bombing tournament in Las Vegas USA against several other wings in the USAFE and USAF which the 81st won with honours.

RAF Manston was tarnished by a very nasty shooting incident in which an Air Force policeman went 'berserk' on the base, shooting at random individuals and causing causalities, some fatal. He then left the base to go down town, where he was soon apprehended by the British police. A very unhappy and distressing time for everyone.

The move would see three or four small **C-123 Provider** aircraft flying between bases to airlift all the squadron equipment along the coast between Orfordness and Ramsgate. The south side of the base would now be more busy than ever and we were still having to 'await the green light' to cross the active runway to get to work. With the munitions areas and the dogs and the additional squadron on the south side, the pressure was on to fund and action that urgently-needed perimeter road.

The 92nd now settled in their squadron buildings, such as they were, just tin huts and Butler sheds. Flush toilets had now been installed with septic tanks to be pumped out by our contractor Mr Turner instead of him working on honey buckets. M41 stoves were installed to combat the frosty conditions that Bentwaters experienced every winter.

Another move was made in 1958. The 78th Squadron moved from Shepherds Grove to RAF Woodbridge to share the base with the 79th from the 20th TFW that have settled in from Upper Heyford. Again we must assume that the move would bring about a cost saving and would give the 81st Wing more immediate local control. The two squadrons at Woodbridge would operate for their respective Wings as they operated different aircraft in different operational roles.

More married family housing was now becoming available and it was clear that with the highest number of quarters at Woodbridge it made sense to erect the main schools there.

In the meantime, with no High School on either base, the elder teenage schoolboys and girls would be offered places in London or Germany. The teenagers would have to stay over between Monday and Friday, the distance between bases being too great for daily travel. Other US Air Force families would provide temporary accommodation for the teenagers; they were very good at helping out in this way.

The 78th Squadron personnel working at their new base at Woodbridge would have a long daily haul back to their Married Family Housing 'Tobacco Bungalows' that were now finished and occupied by the Shepherds Grove American families.

Shepherds Grove base would eventually be closed to military activity and vacated and offered to the local council for disposal, including the bungalows and technical buildings that would be offered to light industry.

We were now well into 1958 and both the 81st FBW and 20th FBW would take on board changes to the type of aircraft that they would be operating in the 60s.

A VIP visit and coach tour of the base was arranged for the UK Minister of Defence, Mr George Ward. Amongst other things his attention would be drawn to the need for a Bentwaters bypass. Plans had been made and the Americans would no doubt express their anxiety about how close the public was to the airfield boundary, particularly at Wood Barn corner. Special funding would be requested for this urgent project.

The 81st would change aircraft from F-84 Thunderstreaks to the more advanced F-101 Voodoo and the 20th FBW would get the F-100 Super Sabre. Both these aircraft would introduce *reheat power thrust afterburners* for take-off and *drag chute* braking assistance. A much improved type of aircraft but more noise could be expected from these more powerful and faster machines.

Colonel James R. DuBose Jr would assume Wing Commander duties from May 1960 for two months after the departure of Harry Crouch. Harry had been Wing Commander for three years during most of that time. My wife Lottie had helped Mrs Crouch with the household chores and not once did Harry pass the time of day with her. He even left it to Mrs Crouch to apologise for him. Ah well, it takes all sorts to keep this world turning...

There was a terrible accident in December 1958 involving the 79th Squadron based at Woodbridge under the direction of the Upper Heyford 20th Fighter Bomber Wing. A Super Sabre F-100 jet aircraft crashed at Kesgrave onto a caravan sales complex. A woman working in the office was killed and several other members of staff were injured. The pilot of the aircraft, Lieutenant Charles Prescot, baled out and landed safely. The Sabre engine was on fire as it lifted off the Woodbridge runway. Coming just after Xmas this was a real blow for everyone and demonstrated the dangers we all faced.

The new bungalow being constructed down at the bottom of Site 5, with a pair of 4-bedroom houses opposite, was nearly complete and with Colonel (later Major-General) Eugene Strickland taking the Wing in July 1960 for two years, he and his family would take up residence in the new Quarters 621, with my wife Lottie helping his lovely wife Marian. Opposite, in one of the new four-bedroom houses (Quarters 620A) would be occupied by Colonel Risher, Chief of Wing Supplies. The Rishers were a large family by today's standards, 10 in all, so the large house was a godsend to them.

We now had tin huts between both new housing sites. The huts could not come down just at the moment as airmen's living quarters were in short supply. The new Airmen's Barracks was now in place at Site 8 and a new Dining Hall was constructed adjacent with an offloading ramp that was forever holding three feet of rainwater where again the drainage was inadequate. This part of the base was very heavy clay soil and drainage was always a problem. A flood pump was eventually installed to everyone's satisfaction.

'The Way They See Us' – 1950s/60s

Bentwaters had now been occupied by the USAF for 10 years so it was possible that some of those who had come over in the early 50s were back doing a second tour. I have been fortunate to find **Stanley J. Pytel**, a Voodoo pilot who was here flying F-86 Sabre jets in the early 50s and returned in the 1960s with the F-101 Voodoo. Stan doesn't pull any punches when it comes to describing us Brits and our funny ways but I'm sure any Brit reading this will take it in good part, while Stan's fellow Americans will no doubt empathise with his frustrations.

AS A PARTICIPANT/OBSERVER the author has had the opportunity to study the actions and interactions of an American group in a foreign society. For 3½ years residence was established 'on the economy' [off the military installation]. After a three-year interval in the United States, three more years were spent in the same English locality but this time habitat was established among other American families on base.

Great Britain has had many Americans in her midst but never on the scale that was begun in 1951. When NATO took advantage of the World's largest aircraft carrier, it transferred hundreds of USAF aircraft, thousands of support personnel and their families to the land of warm beer and cold houses.

On a hazy autumn day the fighter interceptor unit that I belonged to alighted at RAF Station Bentwaters, Suffolk, England, after an Interesting island hopping flight across the North Atlantic. Hundreds of dependents followed their sponsors two to six months later, depending on the availability of housing.

HOUSING

From 1951 to 1958, Yank families lived among the natives in a variety of shelters: some big, some small, some old, some new, but all having one thing in common – a lack of heat. For a group used to being warm, Suffolk's housing proved a real challenge to housewives and husbands unaccustomed to wearing woollies and servicing a variety of mobile heating equipment – whose only common feature was that it was located in the centre of the room. The number of rooms in a house could be determined from outside by counting the number of chimney pots because every room except the bathroom had a fireplace. You could always tell where a Yank lived because the windows were closed and taped.

After considerable house hunting, most Yanks came to the conclusion that the English dislike cooking and rarely bathe. Kitchens were usually small and poorly equipped, many houses lacked bath tubs and showers were non-existent. Most baths had Chippendale (ball and claw footed) bathtubs located with the wash basin in a room separate from the WC (water closet). 'Closet' meant 'toilet', so many a Yank was chided by estate agents when commenting on the lack of closets [clothes cupboards].

In the more progressive homes, novel arrangements for heating water, considered very modern by the natives, were found over bathtubs and sinks. These gas or electric water heaters were called 'geysers'. They sputtered and fumed over the tub or kitchen sink, terrorizing many a spoiled American housewife until more suitable accommodations were found.

We expended much time, energy, and money attempting to bring the home comforts to what we thought was a satisfactory level. I am sure that many Englishmen thought we were daft.

Woollies-clad British visitors invariably found our houses uncomfortably warm and lightly clad Yanks indulged in more hot tea and biscuits than usual while visiting their English friends.

In 1951 the after effects of the War were still sharply evident in the shortages and use of ration books. Grocery shopping was a social ritual involving several shops: bread from the baker; fresh vegetables from the greengrocer; meat, except bacon, from the butcher; bacon, eggs and tinned goods from the grocer.

Refrigerators, sneeringly referred to as 'American gadgets', were tiny and scarce, thus marketing was a daily routine. Queues were common. Often the long lines of patient 'locals' and impatient Americans were disappointed when, arriving at the head of the line, they found that a particular cut of bacon had been sold and the attendant would not bother to cut anymore until he was good and ready. "Come back later, dear." Punch put it very well saying, The English people lack stamina and would rarely queue for more than two hours – by that time some hot-head at the back of the line is likely to inquire as to what is going on at the head of the line."

Until a Base Commissary was established, living on the economy was an adventure for some — a source of constant complaint for others and a health hazard for all of us foreigners. British beef often came from cattle that were not TB inspected, many local dairies did not pasteurise their milk and the local

farmers' use of night soil on their vegetable gardens caused our perhaps over-anxious medics to recommend soaking fresh salad vegetables in a bacteria killing chemical solution.

This was a nuisance, causing many to resort to the more practical and pleasant expedient bug-killing via large and frequent doses of low-proof alcoholic beverages. We were, and still are, accused of drinking to excess, but, like the French, fustify it on a health basis.

Normally the US Forces were adequately provided for at overseas stations, but urgency precluded establishment of amenities peculiar to a group of Americans settling down for at least three years in an unusual environment. A small exchange (BX) provided the troops with basic necessities such as cigarettes, soap, and prophylactics, but nylons and toilet tissue (except for the waxed British variety) were not available for months – and then these luxuries arrived in dribbles.

The mail order business boomed during my first tour (1951-55) and continues today, though somewhat abated by bigger and better exchanges. Our Sears 'wish book' never ceased to be marvelled at by our working-class neighbours and, although we were frequently criticized for our dress, near the end of this first tour Roebuck jeans were noticed among the younger indigenous members of this population.

FUNCTIONS

As a member of NATO's air arm from 1951 to 1955, this group was unique in that it was NATO's only operational interceptor unit equipped with supersonic aircraft. In cooperation with the RAF, the American Sabres were primarily responsible for the air defence of the UK.

The Yanks took their mission seriously but were often frustrated by the necessary evils often imposed upon a sub-culture. Though we financed the lion's share of the base maintenance and construction, final decisions as to time, place and materials were made by the UK Air Ministry. Runway construction, always vital to effective mission accomplishment, appeared to us to proceed at a snail's pace.

What with 'elevenses', tea, strong unions, and outmoded equipment, the delays in what we considered crash programs were the source of some of our strongest criticisms.

An operational problem of great concern was that of reaction time in an emergency situation. With personnel scattered from three to forty winding miles away, telephonic alerting was an absolute necessity and our British friends agreed, but at the end of three years our reaction time was still unacceptably slow – many airmen were still waiting for telephones from the British government-owned telephone company. From 1959 to 1962, with base housing and Big Brother (alerting squawk box) hanging on the living room wall, practice alerts came frequently, frightening wives and children but reducing reaction time to a satisfactory level. Once airborne we worked smoothly and efficiently with the RAF – our differences began and ended on the ground.

Social activities as a group were limited during my first tour by distance from the Club, but squadron get-togethers were frequent enough to maintain close relationships within the group. A definite advantage (though some Americans disagreed) of not having base housing was the opportunity to mix with the local community's inhabitants – be it a pint of beer at the local, tea with a neighbour, or a foursome at the nearby golf course.

The advent of base housing resulted in social functions resembling those of a ghetto. The base became self-sufficient to the extent that the physical, religious, intellectual and social needs of the majority were met within the confines of the installation. It is regrettable that some Americans never ranged further than the nearest village during their three-year tour. A formal Anglo-American relations organization was functioning but, from my observations, I found that its tendency to cater to the officer corps limited whatever understanding might have been achieved to a very small part of the American group.

In the early fifties education of American children depended on British schools, public or private. My friends had mixed opinions of British education. They whose children went to public (our private) schools were satisfied; others, fearing adjustment problems, couldn't wait for the American schools to open on base. Secondary school children posed a special problem in that they were forced to leave home to attend American High Schools in London or Munich, or private schools in England or Switzerland. These students commuted weekends or at the ends of semesters, depending upon the distance.

CULTURAL INTERACTIONS

Prior to our departure for England, an oft-mentioned advantage of duty there was the lack of a language barrier. To the surprise of many, communication between cultures enjoying a common language was often difficult and sometimes very misleading.

The desk clerk of a Southampton hotel was only being courteous when he asked the American school teachers, "What time would you like to be knocked up in the morning, ladies?"

Our use of the word 'napkin' upset many a Maître D of London's finest restaurants until education of both sides resolved what was once an embarrassing situation. On my first tour the degrading terms "bloody and "bloke" were politely avoided but recent experience found these words used surprisingly often by both British and Americans.

One particularly impressive feature of English is its precision. The ironmonger, when asked about 'weather stripping', had never heard of it. After hearing its description, he beamed and said, "Oh, you mean *draft excluder*." Disdaining our propensity for superlatives, the British simply add a qualifying word as the need arises. For example, when we developed a radio frequency higher than VHF (very high frequency) we promptly labelled it UHF (ultra high frequency) whereas the English called it VHFI (very high frequency indeed).

The guttural accents of typical Suffolk folk were as hard to understand as that of Father Jolly, the village priest, whose sermons in a thick Oxford accent required keen attention for minimal comprehension. I thought that after nine years a noticeable improvement in communication had been achieved but doubt returned while reading an article in *Punch* which attempted to clarify such American expressions as these:

"Are you kidding?" meaning "The information you have given me is superfluous."

"A Rat race" meaning "any lucrative calling."

"This is coffee?" meaning "There are many points of difference between our two ways of life."

SOCIAL CUSTOMS

Perhaps the most conspicuous difference between the two cultures was dress.

"You can tell a Yank a mile away," the British would say, and more often than not they were right. Who else but a Yank would venture out in public in tight jeans, loud jackets and fluorescent socks and ties? Recognition was easy in the fifties but not so in the sixties because by then the American influence on the young Briton's attire was obvious. What is not widely publicized is the influence conservative American clothing fashions have had.

According to *Punch* the spotless light topcoat or Macintosh now seen in London is a result of the American concern for fashion. A casualty of this change has been the filthy old masculine 'Mac' that was an honourable possession. In the early fifties, American women eager to fill their wardrobes with English woollens were disappointed to find severe classic styles limited in size and colour. Most ready-mades came in shades of black, navy, grey ("nigger" and "donkey" as advertised). Sizes were measured from the nape of the neck to the hem and strategic dimensions were swallowed up in two general categories: *women's size* (baggy) and *outsize* (huge).

Small women were advised to visit the girls' department, where they found the traditional school tunic in the sedate colours plus two juvenile tones – deep maroon and bottle green. Knit dresses and suits, having been custom made in a dazzling array of colours, were almost uniform among American wives and the styles of Sears Roebuck and Montgomery Ward were cherished.

The situation was greatly alleviated during my first tour, not just because of American pressure but because British women also were fed up with the "make-do" (do nothing) policy of post-war Britain and demanded more variety from clothing manufacturers. In the sixties even the lower priced stores had an endless array of attractive clothing, some of which seemed avant-garde with direct influence from the continent and Hollywood.

The most shocking change was seeing British women wear slacks in public. In the fifties they had always been properly, if dowdily, dressed, except when they visited continental ski or beach resorts. The British, especially the young, quite obviously drowned their reserve in the Channel when they went "on holiday," or perhaps the bright, dry sunshine of the mountains and Riviera dried up their "Nanny is watching" mentality.

In the early fifties American housewives were criticized mainly because they were 'spoiled' – desiring such 'gadgets' as central heating, refrigerators, washing machines and ovens large enough to roast a turkey (the British had theirs roasted at the baker's). They were so 'spoiled' that they found firing and cleaning the numerous hearths and portable heaters time consuming and tedious, as well as being a hazard to toddlers. Other strong criticisms concerned their conspicuous dress, lack of control of children, and aggressiveness while shopping.

Having had a lifetime of serve-yourself shopping, they found it difficult to queue patiently while one clerk dashed about the shop, sometimes going to bins outside on the sidewalk, to select each customer's daily purchases. The British were too polite to tell the Americans they mustn't pick up items from the sidewalk bins on their way into the shops, but raised eyebrows, loamy stares, and an occasional word via the children's grapevine got messages across. Shop clerks always said "thank you" or its condensation "ta" after individually fetching each item. A frigid 'ta' translated into Brooklynese meant "Pleez don't squeeze da banana" although our gaily-clad, noisy children were as great a jolt upon the English scene as the screaming jet engines and sonic booms of the cookie-pushing Anglo-American relations committees.

Warm, heartfelt friendships were made when schoolfriends brought their parents together or when a "Nanny" or even a stranger in the street fell in love with a "bonnie babe". Numerous American children, when stateside, received hand-knit woollies and tins of biscuits from devoted English friends, some of who could scarcely afford to pay the postage. Friendships, like most other British commodities, were not quickly, but strongly, made. We Yanks missed drive-ins as well as twenty-four hour restaurants and bars but we got into the picnic basket, thermos and six-pack habit. In the sixties we enjoyed drinking American beer from "tins with those peculiar triangular holes" but during our first tour they preferred drinks at blood temperature – in a glass.

In the sixties London flaunted many first-class restaurants, most of which served continental cuisine – at continental prices. In the early fifties no Americans were eager to eat out, except that it was cheaper than eating at home to the mercenary Yanks. Limited eating and drinking hours seemed to be poor business and the 'lunch hours' and 'early closing days' of all village shops were outright madness. The shops closed promptly at 1:00 pm and remained closed until 2:00 or 2:30, depending upon what extent lunch hour the proprietor required. No matter what price purchase was hanging fire at 12:59, customers were given the "Call back after lunch, dear" treatment and ushered out, unable to force the money and extra minute's attention upon the storekeeper.

During my second tour, several shops in many villages were eager to grab the lunch hour trade and super-markets appeared in two fairly large communities.

AUTOS AND CYCLES

A British driver's license was required of all those other than tourists in the UK. American servicemen received them upon presentation of current US licenses but their wives and other dependents had to pass a written and especially difficult driving test. Many wives failed two and three times and some never did pass. Those who failed or feared the test but wanted to drive took advantage of the one-year tourist grace period over three successive years by crossing the Channel at the nearest port once a year and getting their passports stamped on re-entry to the UK. This legal but questionable practice may have had some bearing on our high auto accident rate in the UK.

A source of continual friction between the Yanks and the British were the big American automobiles. In 1951 when I insured my 1949 Ford with a British firm, full coverage charges were under sixty dollars, but three years later the rates had skyrocketed to sixty dollars for liability alone. Our 'huge' limousines with the driver on the wrong side just did not fit the typical British country road. The roads were narrow, high crowned, often shoulder less and winding – an automotive environment directly opposite to what our machines were designed for. These roadway features, along with fog and alcohol, resulted in record accident rates. Special programs in cooperation with the local constabulary were instituted in an attempt to reduce auto accidents but, though accidents were reduced in number, insurance costs remained high.

In the early fifties British auto manufacturers were similar to Henry FordI, in that a purchaser could choose any colour of auto as long as it was black. Along with our gaudy taste in clothes, we were criticized for garish auto colour schemes. There was a marked change in the late fifties, however, and today the all-black British vehicle is in the minority, along with semaphore-type direction signals and single headlight operation in the dim position. England's long-awaited acceptance of 'hire purchase' (instalment buying) put many more autos on the road in the sixties than in the fifties.

Cyclists were numerous in Britain and the cycling situation is one of the important items covered in orientation lectures for recent arrivals. Unaccustomed to coping with cyclists on the highways and byways, sometimes three and four deep, with side-cars, yet Yanks were cautioned to honour the cyclist's right of way. An American car negotiating a blind curve must steer close to the edge when an oncoming Yank auto was met. In this situation the narrow, shoulder-less road left little or no room for the cyclist. Few Americans cycled. Those who did – my wife and me included – were considered "rather curious" by their English friends and accused of "going bloke" by their American compatriots.

CONFLICTS

When a society as tradition-bound and conservative as the British has within it a highly motivated progressive group which is generally technologically superior, criticism and resentment were inevitable results. As a group we didn't and still don't realize the sociological ramifications of a former colony's patronizing attitude toward a once superior mother country. This attitude was reflected in our frequent and often thoughtless comparisons. They had one superhighway in 1960, we had many; we have a fetish for cleanliness and sanitation, they enjoy fish and chips served in old newspaper; they use hand labour at every opportunity, we mechanize for the smallest task; most of their restaurants were disappointing, ours compare favourably with the best in the world; they have little or no central heating, almost every American home is centrally heated; their plumbing is ridiculous with water pipes and drains attached to the walls on the outside of the houses and "pull the chain to flush" type commodes, our plumbing is way superior, brought on by a lack of knowledge or skill in such tasks as trying to build a fire or repeated embarrassingly noisy attempts to flush a toilet.

We received our share of criticism also, most of which, in typical Yank fashion, was shrugged off as "sour grapes". British complaints were summed up in the old chestnut, "Overpaid, oversexed, and over here." They ridiculed our "boorish behaviour" (we nonchalantly did things that "aren't done") and our "outlandish attire" (men stripped to the waist on the golf course and wives shopping in slacks and curlers – shocking!) Our speech was referred to as "the transatlantic twang" lacking in precision and in pronunciation. We were too aggressive and lacked reserve. We emphasized materialism at the expense of intellectualism. They said Americans "would go down in history as plumbers".

Although a wide difference existed, the gap in understanding was narrowing. Mutual benefits had been gained through intermarriage, charitable works, British patience, gains in education (it is impossible to avoid history), cultural enrichment

(London theatres and concert halls were two hours away and relatively inexpensive), an image of America other than the Hollywood version, a British financial gain of over 400 million dollars annually, clothing styles, and most important of all, understanding. The Hollywood stereotype of America was broken and the history book version of England was brought into the clear focus of reality.

In common with many Yanks we enjoyed our two tours in Britain and have made lasting friendships. Muriel Muddock, who has since passed away, became part of our family as our live-in nanny. She was so attached to our youngest daughter, a toddler, that when she died she willed her detached cottage in Wickham Market to My Sal.

❖ ❖ ❖

Thanks Stan, Most enjoyable.

Joe Williams' F-84 Thunderstreak receiving attention [JW].

79th Squadron based at RAF Woodbridge change aircraft to the Super Sabre F-100. [GP]

A 'Voodoo' in flight over Suffolk. [CW]

The long-awaited Bentwaters by-pass road opens, 1961.

Twin Bases Developed – 1960s

At this point we should appreciate that a very large and expensive building programme was being planned for the Twin Bases. 1959/60 saw the completion of an A&E (Armament and Electronic) facility over on the South Side of the airfield. The A&E was where we would see dust-free floors from where high tech equipment would be worked on in the jet age. Also over on the South Side, № 4 Butler Shed, which the USAF Engineers constructed on the old concrete hard stands last year, would be used by one of the squadrons as an operations room, of which our friend and part author Stan Pytel was a squadron member on F101 Voodoos. Also erected was a steel framed sound suppressor that would serve as a deflector when the aircraft engines were put to the test after an engine refit and before flight testing. This sound deflector would direct the sound skywards but did not entirely take the annoyingly deafening sound of an engine on full power away from the local population, which would prove to be a source of contention for many years to come.

The whole of the Tech Site around the Hangar 45 area was to get main sewage drainage, which would cause upheaval for many months to come.

The old cottage that Lottie and I were living in, just inside the main gate, would be included in this upgrade; they would construct a bathroom on the side of the house, so we were really feeling very pleased with our little lot. The drawback was to be realized later when we used the new bathroom with a portable oil heater to help increase the temperature and there was so much condensation. Well that was to be expected I suppose as they had cut the cost of the bathroom extension by building it in only half brick thick walls, letting the driving rain penetrate to the inside. The old cottages were not subject to building regulations in those days.

I was pressing on with my own Bungalow construction (DIY) so as far as I was concerned and with the help of my work mates Lou Neville and Ron, things were taking shape down at Friday Street, where Lottie, Jenny and I would take up residence in the early 1960s.

It now appeared that the visit by the (Minister of Defence) George Ward a few months earlier was bearing fruit. The construction of the Bentwaters by-pass had begun and in a few months the new roundabout would be in use. There would be no ribbon-cutting ceremony, the old Half Mile Road and Wood Barn Corner section would be closed to the public and the water main to Tunstall would be safe from vehicle damage as the old highway filled up with leaves and became a no-go zone.

The Voodoos were now flying at every opportunity in twos and fours and according to Jim Gibler, one of the pilots who had flown many different aircraft, the Voodoo was a good all-round fighter/bomber serving NATO. Jim Gibler and his family resided in Orford for a considerable time while Jim served at the base. As a result Jim's wife Sally-Ann made friends with a few of the local Orford folk, in particular Mrs Joan Bantoft who in 2004 was still with us at the grand age of 94. Her sons were ready to remind her of those friendly days in the 1950s/60s when the American families enjoyed the English village life. Sadly Sally Ann is no longer with us.

In August 1959 Voodoo crashed at Woodbridge Base. Few details were available about the F-101 coming down onto the runway. Sadly, although the pilot, Lieutenant Sterling H. Lee, baled out he was killed.

Remember Mason Hier, the American who delivered the truck from Burtonwood (the American supply depot in Cheshire) to Bentwaters in 1951? Well, he was back in America with his British wife going about his military business when his commander told him he was posted to a place in the UK called Bentwaters and asked, "Do you know it?"

"Yes Sir, I've been there, so no problem," came the reply.

Mason served at Bentwaters in 1959/61 and again in 1967/71.

The new Bentwaters by-pass opened, much to everyone's delight, none more so than the security police, who were always aware that the old road was too close to the airfield activities for good security. In addition, the new roundabout would help traffic flow and release the traffic control policeman formerly on duty at the crossroads with the Tech Site.

It would be a little further for Lottie to go to catch the school car for Jennie and the bus to town but other than that an improvement all round, with a wider and straighter road for safety.

An important facility on the base which saw its full share of activity was the Base Gym. This was a very large SECO building that stood at the corner of the same site as the tennis courts. There were classrooms behind and at the top of the site stood the Chapel. The Gym would give a great deal of service before a new sports centre was constructed a few years later.

The Bowling Alley, a four-lane facility located adjacent the Tobacco Bungalows, was to be replaced with a much larger facility adjacent the Dining Hall. This would be a very worthwhile new facility where the 81st could really get into competition with other visiting bowling teams.

With the increase in Wing personnel it was becoming clear that the facilities already designed and constructed would need extending. The contractors (Sadler of Ipswich) had moved onto Site 5 to remove the old tin huts and construct 25 new Married Quarters There would be 24 houses as opposed to bungalows and one Wing Commanders bungalow to be built adjacent to the new bungalow Quarters 621 at the end of the site. Colonel Strickland would take the new larger bungalow on its completion.

These new houses would accommodate most of the senior officers needed immediately for Wing support in case of emergency. The contract would run for about a year, English weather permitting, with occupation taking place in 1962. This would bring the total number of MOD Married Quarters at Bentwaters to just 68 – so a large number of airmen would still be living off base for several years to come.

Another open day was arranged. We seemed to be having these every summer. The Voodoo would feature strongly on this day. The presence of a large number of British Police Constables was very noticeable. They were not with the crowd but were sitting in what looked like converted cattle trucks with seats down either side. We learnt that this was because a large number of "Ban the Bomb" protesters were expected.

It was important that the day was not spoilt by these people who were nevertheless allowed onto the airfield to demonstrate their objection to the nuclear weapons carried by the USAF aircraft stationed at Bentwaters, although this armament had been approved by NATO members. Well, it was nice that they could express their views in the Free World. I did not hear of any arrests so I presume they behaved themselves.

The RAF Lightnings put on a show for the Open Day crowd.

These Public Open days would bring different aerobatic teams each year. One year we had the Blue Diamonds – about a dozen Hawker Hunters – which gave a very good display. On another occasion we had 22 Black Hunters which rolled in one complete unit. Some flying, that was!

Then we had the Lightnings, with their chequered yellow and black tail markings. They made a lot of noise and, unbeknown to them, a bit of a problem. They were flying very low – too low, in fact. As they went east to west they stayed down that little bit extra distance and not only bent the TV aerial pole on Fred Page's house with the downdraft they caused but also blew the soot down his chimney to fill the sitting room. It spoilt Fred's day and he spoilt the RAF Commander's day by demanding that someone attend the house immediately to sort out the tragic mess.

The cottages at the end of the runway on Friday Street were not pleasant to live in once the Air Ministry had extended the runway westwards. This had the effect bringing the planes down to an unacceptably low level as they came in to land. But still the MoD chose not to help the occupants.

The Woodbridge Base was not opened to the public. Bentwaters served as the prime base for open days although Woodbridge would host the odd Sports Open Day since they were the venue for American Football matches between the 81st Wing team and teams from the other US Wings in the UK. At the Woodbridge base there were wide open spaces that could be utilised for sports activities for the base schools and service personnel. With such a high number of married quarters now being occupied at Woodbridge, a number of play areas were planned and built.

Woodbridge Base would also be the venue for small arms training. At the northwest corner across the runway a range was installed with all the safety barriers needed for public safety in the adjoining forest. This range would be a busy place as the airmen kept up with their small arms practice. The clay pigeon range at the Rod & Gun Club at Bentwaters was purely a leisure pursuit.

Woodbridge now had its own chapel and service station with fuel at US prices. A small shop was also now active at Woodbridge, although the main shopping would be at

Bentwaters. A shuttle bus service ran frequently throughout the day between the two bases via Eyke village.

The Commissary at Bentwaters was now offering a variety of different foods and the BX was able to provide household goods and clothing to help make life for the US personnel a bit more like home. My wife and I came to like the word 'Delicatessen'.

There was now an Elementary School at Woodbridge and a High School was being planned. Belles Coaches and Galloway Coaches were running to and from the school complex to convey children who lived as far afield as Walberswick, Thorpeness, Aldeburgh and Orford to the east and Ipswich to the west.

In September 1961 there was an aircraft crash at Bentwaters which involved another Voodoo. As the F-101 was approaching the 08 East End runway the pilot lost control and, missing the touchdown area, the aircraft landed on the grass on the south side and veered towards the place where vehicle traffic was waiting to cross the runway (which, as I have explained, was the only way to get from one side of the airfield to the other. It goes without saying that this was somewhere that we did not want a runaway aircraft to appear. A Sergeant who was waiting at the traffic lights in his car and a small child passenger in another car were killed as the Voodoo swept across the old disused runway and headed towards the newly constructed Butler sheds, where my friend Stan was working.

Here is his story of what happened next.

Voodoo Crash into 92nd Fighter Squadron Operations

It was late August or early September, 1961. So far no one has come up with the pilot's name. He had just reported to the squadron within the week. This might have been his first flight at Bentwaters. The F-101 crashed during final approach to runway 08 at RAF Station Bentwaters, Suffolk, England. The

pilot was new to this aircraft and we thought he was experiencing pitch-up, an out of control manoeuvre which occurs when a nose-up pitch altitude is exceeded.

Thinking that he was in pitch-up, the pilot ejected at a very low altitude – too low for parachute deployment. He was fatally injured. The aircraft crashed slightly south of the runway, struck some privately owned vehicles parked near 92nd Ops and seriously injured one of our pilots who was in the path of the burning aircraft. It continued across the parking area and crashed into the 92nd Ops building.

I was in the ops office briefing two pilots on a flight they were planning when we heard a loud Whoomp! Looking out the window we saw a large ball of fire heading our way. All three of us dove under the desk. When the debris stopped falling we evacuated the area, receiving just a few scratches.

Besides the loss of a pilot and serious injury to another, the squadron lost all of its pilots' flying records. It was weeks before duplicate records were received from the States. We moved our ops into an adjoining building, with little disruption of flying activities.

Nice one Stan. Thank you.

The twin bases were increasing in size and personnel. Additional barrack blocks were being constructed which were now a three-storey construction but still with the centre corridor much disliked by the troops.

There was no doubt that the sewage treatment plants on both bases would have to be extended with more drying beds and improved effluent drainage. Woodbridge, having sandy soil, would handle the extra discharge with the extending of the open ditches. Bentwaters, on the other hand, would require an extra-large project. The open ditches here were overflowing onto the road that led to the Hall Gardens from Ivy Lodge, a very unsatisfactory state of affairs as

A Voodoo well bedded-in at Bentwaters. [USAF]

far as the locals were concerned. The cure would be to pipe the effluent over 1 mile to the River Deben at Loudham.

The water supply for Bentwaters was proving inadequate so a second borehole was drilled 100 yards away from the existing one. The original Bentwaters borehole had been deepened from 70 to 140 feet to avoid drying up but this proved unsuccessful. The Anglian Water Board were unable to supply Bentwaters with water because they had a full commitment, which included the Orfordness Island "Cobra Mist" project.

One problem with the water from the Bentwaters boreholes was the high alkaline content which caused a corrosion problem with the steel piping and in addition was not responding to softening as we had hoped.

By 1962 Colonel Strickland had now settled into the new larger bungalow with its very large, plush lounge. It had taken a while to get to this stage and many bucks, but we now had a Commander's residence that was worthy of a Wing Chief, where Wing Commanders could entertain VIP guests. In the summer of this same year Colonel Strickland would move to Germany on promotion to Brigadier- General whereupon Colonel William C. Clark took over the Wing for the next few months.

My family had now moved house after 13 years living at the old cottage just inside the base. It was time to move on and take on this thing called a mortgage. We had occupied the old cottage at midnight on our wedding day – May 27th 1950 – with not a sole on the base. Mrs Toller was next door and we had our wedding present – the little Cairn Terrier.

1963 would see an extension of the Bentwaters water supply lines including high-level water storage tanks adjacent the BCE office on the Tech Site and over the airfield two storage tanks adjacent the hangar Building 74. Unfortunately, the water pressure to many of the facilities was very poor, which the Fire Department demanded be increased as soon as possible.

Many more new facilities were coming on stream, including an Aircraft Wash Rack and additional warehousing with concrete loading ramps adjacent the BCE Office on the Tech Site.

We had another wedding in the lovely summer of 1963 when Ron Burrell married Pamela Ling at the village church in Snape. I've kept in touch with Ron and he recalled the wedding when I e-mailed him in 2003, 40 years on. This is what he wrote:

Happy Thanksgiving from Colorado USA. We are fine. Don't know if we shall be able to walk after eating all that turkey and trimmings. Another tradition started by our British cousins. Wedding in 1963? Oh yes I remember now. My mother didn't want me to marry a British girl. I then asked, "Why did you marry Dad? He was from Shropshire. He sneaked into the US back in 1915.

My English Mum-in-Laws famous words after visiting the family home in Snape were, "Huh! Get rid of that bloke. We don't want any Bloody Yanks here." I had to laugh when I saw her face after I told her I was a British American. Her face was a picture.

I reckon that she had some hard feelings from the war years when the Americans overran all the villages and towns. They certainly left their mark on the countryside. I understand that there were more children of American descent in East Anglia than all of Britain. I know several people who live there whose father was American.

Hope to make a trip back in 2004. I nearly retired but decided not to. So I am still working at the post office. Some sucker has to do it.

Ron and Pam Burrell

Thanks Ron and Pam. Nice one.

In August 1963 we welcomed a new Wing Commander, Colonel (later Major-General) Robin Olds. Colonel Olds was no stranger to the UK; he had served here during World War II, flying Mustangs from Duxford.

Colonel Olds and his wife Mrs Ella Olds would spend two years with us after they moved into the new bungalow that had been christened by the Stricklands and would now be turned into a very different looking residence inside as Ella, a former actress, introduced changes. She liked white and, to our horror, requested that all the woodgrain finished doors be painted white, including the room divider on which a live plant was growing. Ah well, it takes all sorts.

Before becoming Mrs Olds, Ella had been Ella Reins, a relation I'm informed, of the actor Claude Reins. It was noticeable when one was inside the Wing Commander's quarters, checking electrical or plumbing

faults, that pictures of the actress in her heyday were very evident – some from the 1940s magazines *Illustrated* and *Picture Post*. Robin, on the other hand, became a very good Voodoo pilot and soon demonstrated on Open Day – with three other pilots as an aerobatic foursome – how well the aircraft performed.

A very prominent figure at this time who I have to tell you about was the Deputy Director of Operations Lieutenant Colonel (later 4-Star General) Daniel 'Chappie' James.[1] He was well over 6 feet tall and one of the heavyweights, as a pilot could be, a very efficient and professional officer who occupied the bungalow in the village of Chillesford, to the east of the base.

I remember Chappie James on Open Day sitting on a chair on the Control Tower balcony giving the entire air show commentary; a good show Colonel! The weather helped on that day as Colonel Olds demonstrated the Voodoo with his four-aircraft display team.

One occasion comes to mind when Chappie James was making enquiries about a Dakota aircraft which had skidded off the runway as it was taking off. Heff and Brian, the airfield electricians, were approached by Chappie James to ask if they had seen anything unusual, to which Heff replied, "I wish we could help but no, we didn't see anything."

It turned out that the rudder or flap locks were still in their locking position; someone in the groundcrew had forgotten to remove them, which resulted in the Dakota aborting on take-off the way it did. It could have been much worse. From now on all these locks were fitted with trailing red flags that could be easily seen from afar.

Chappie James was one of over 900 African American US Air Force pilots, 450 of

---

[1] Chappie James made the air force his career and became the USAF's first African American Four Star General. Sadly, he died after enjoying a very short time in retirement.

81ˢᵗ Wing Commander Colonel Olds and his wife head the welcome at a New Year's Day Reception. [USAF]

whom served in the North Africa, Sicily and European WW2 campaigns. The Germans called them *"Schwartze Vogelmenshen"* (Black Birdmen).

My wife Lottie was again working in the smaller bungalow next door with the Alexanders, where she had been formerly with the Strickland family. Mrs Betty Alexander had to take her driving test in Ipswich. She didn't pass but was returning soon to the States, so it wasn't too big a setback.

Mrs Olds (Ella) was looking to employ a live-in maid but Lottie was very happy helping the Base Commander Colonel Alexander and his wife. As far as I know Ella was never able to get a live-in maid. The Olds certainly knew how to put on a party. Ella was a great hostess and everything was perfect in this great new bungalow.

November 1963 would bring an event that shook the world. Everyone would recall

exactly where they were when they heard the news that President John F. Kennedy had been assassinated, none more so than the US personnel at Bentwaters and Woodbridge.

Betty Alexander recalls her own words as: "We shall never be able to hold our heads up again."

The shock was earth shaking and every serviceman looked to the Wing Commander to see his course of action. The Air Ministry were approached to prepare an area of the Chapel garden for the planting of a conifer tree and a support stand for a plaque that would be placed in the West Side Chapel garden. After a few days preparation an open air service was held with a very large gathering of USAF senior officers accompanied by local council members and other dignitaries.

A tree was planted at the Chapel in memory of JFK, 1963. [MH]

It was a very shocking time, even for us British civilian staff, who felt that we too had lost someone we were close to.

Shortly afterwards there was another crash. On the approach to the Bentwaters runway from the east over the River Alde this aircraft lost height and was brought down in the marshes behind Iken church. Not a very pleasant situation. The pilot managed to get himself out of the cockpit but was having difficulty in walking through the mud. He was sinking into the swamp but luckily a Mr Mael was in the vicinity and went to assist him and got him to dry land.

It was the 3rd or 4th Voodoo that had come to grief since they arrived at Bentwaters. Things could only get better. The USAF Officers and airmen were very grateful to Mr Mael for assisting the pilot in this difficult terrain and were quick to arrange a presentation on the base for Mr Mael and his immediate family, a very nice gesture by our American friends, who always liked to show their appreciation despite their military reserve.

What we do know is that the pressure was now on to obtain funding for a perimeter road around the runway following the earlier Voodoo crash. It was not safe for traffic to cross the active runway or be parked nearby

while waiting to cross. At Woodbridge they didn't have that problem because everything was on one side of the runway.

A major extension of the weapons area was ongoing at Woodbridge, as well as full scale re-sheeting of two of the old wartime aircraft hangars. A small firefighting helicopter also arrived at Woodbridge but the general feeling was that it was an unnecessary and expensive piece of equipment. Its stay was short.

There were two Squadron Operations buildings at Woodbridge – a SECO at the west end of the airfield and a brick single-storey that was now refurbished and extended and taken over by 78th Squadron. It was strange to see the large snake which was kept in a glass case in the entrance hall. I presumed it was asleep as I viewed it through the glass.

Sadly, the 78th Squadron based at Woodbridge lost an aircraft on 15th May 1964. While flying a training exercise over Scotland the F-101 Voodoo crashed 15 miles west of Fort William and no details were available at the time regarding the pilot.

Much more concrete had been laid to help keep Foreign Object Damage (FOD) to a minimum. Woodbridge base was more susceptible to FOD because of the wide old wartime runway with only the centre 50 yard wide strip in use, which had been over-slabbed and tarmac-coated as the runway proper. The 50yd wide runways each side, known as the 'outfield' and 'infield' were not to be trafficked so as to prevent FOD being brought onto the active aircraft taxiways.

Motor vehicle traffic between bases was increasing. The military had a need to tow small ground equipment to and from each base via Butley village and civilian cars were travelling between bases via Friday Street. This road was very narrow and everyone had to be aware of left hand drive vehicles moving fast around the sharp blind bends.

Meanwhile over at Bentwaters Aircraft Hangar 45 had a metal annex building attached on the north side, which would prove to be very useful for the ground crews to take a break and the Chief Sergeant to do his paperwork. Someone on his staff chose to install a sign over the top of the door with the words:

IF ANYONE LIKES HARD WORK THEY CAN SURE HAVE A HELL OF A TIME HERE.

It was a lovely summer day and the smart young lady who worked behind the counter in the BX or Air Force European Exchange Service (AFEES) as it is now called, was feeling a bit broody and asked her boyfriend, who drove one of the AFEES delivery trucks, to take her out in the sunshine. They knew where they were going, they went there quite regularly, for a drive through Ivy Lodge archway and into the park where there were some lovely cedar trees and grass areas. She didn't object to him removing her bits and bobs and the inevitable happened. The young couple were not aware, however, that my mates were working close by but were not prepared to spoil the young lady's enjoyment. I hope she was not late back to work...

The year was 1965 and in July Colonel Olds was moving on to a Brigadier General's Post and Colonel (later Maj. General) De Witt Richard Searles would assume command of the 81st FBW.

As the Alexanders were also moving back to the States and my wife Lottie would now be joining the Searles family in the large bungalow three times a week to keep the place ship-shape. Everyone settled in to enjoy the next two years. It's worth pointing out that Lottie received her 36th Xmas card (in 2003) from that very nice family. Barbara Searles was a very nice lady and very good company. She was ready to praise those who had been most helpful during their UK tour, particularly Miss Jackie Errington the Personnel Relations Officer, who organised all the meetings with local people in authority. Richard Searles became very friendly with the late Sir Peter Mathew, Chief Constable of the Suffolk Constabulary. The

The Fire Fighting helicopter that was based at Woodbridge – but not for long. [GP]

Wing Commander Dick Searles tries a helmet for size. [USAF]

Wing Commander felt it important to invite such people to the base to cement better relations. I had the pleasure of meeting Sir Peter and Lady Mathew at their home in Liphook, Hampshire and received a very nice letter. Here is part of what Sir Peter said:

Many thanks for the video of The History of Bentwaters. We have just played it right through and it leaves us with happy memories of our short stay in East Suffolk. We were delighted to see a couple of times Dick and Barbara and the short reference to HM The Queen using Bentwaters en route to open the Snape Maltings.

My association with Bentwaters started in May 1968 when I became the Chief Constable of East Suffolk Police. Shortly after I took up office I was invited to the senior officers mess at Bentwaters. The conversation with the senior officers was a wee bit 'stilted'. I doubt if many of them had met a Chief Constable in

the U.K. and must have wondered just what his position was.

After a short time one of the US pilots mentioned Woodbridge base and I said to him "Oh, I landed an Airspeed Oxford there in 1944."

You should have seen the look on his face. "You landed an Oxford at Woodbridge? Were you a pilot?"

I replied "Yes, at that time I was Staff Pilot to two night fighter squadrons in West Raynham, Norfolk and a German Night Fighter had landed by mistake at Woodbridge. The crew were arrested and we wanted to look at their night flying radio gear."

Well, after that I was 'in'.

When the war started I was a PC in the West End of London – the police service was a 'reserved occupation' and apart from those on 'reserve' to the Colours we were not allowed to volunteer for active service. However, after the Blitz on London in February 1941 the then Commissioner allowed us to volunteer and be seconded to the RAF and Fleet Air Arm as pilots or observers. A total of 1,696 of us from London went into the RAF – 383 were killed. From our division in the West End 45 went, 25 were killed and 11 didn't come back and took up other employment, one was medically discharged and only eight of us came back to being constables, like the tale of the ancient mariner.

When Dick Searles took over as Colonel i/c Bentwaters I found that when he was training as a pilot in the USA, on the Senior Flying Course one of his instructors had been one of the London policemen who joined the RAF. We were up to all the mischief you could think of but never were caught. Cunning coppers!

Incidentally, my police sergeant covering Bentwaters was Sgt Airey from Wickham Market. We called him the Chief Constable of Bentwaters. When there was a 'high level' social function Sergeant and Mrs Airey and Margaret and I were always invited. When Colonel Searles was promoted and posted I presented him with a new Suffolk Constabulary helmet and a truncheon, which now adorn his study in McLean.

Our sincerest congratulations Norman on your personal efforts to produce The History of Bentwaters video, a splendid production – I am sure it would be very much appreciated by all those who had the good fortune to be 'associated with Bentwaters'.

Dick, the Officers mess Chef, would go to the big bungalow and attend to the preparing and cooking for the VIPs on these special occasions. Good for US/Anglo relations.

We now had a new Resident Engineer, Mr Slight having replaced Ron Stewart. REs move around the world to all kinds of places. I understood that Ron Stewart had gone to Aden or Nepal. Mr Slight had spent a lifetime on airfield pavement work.

John Mowlem, the airfield pavements contractor, moved onto the base to overslab the hardstandings adjacent the Rod & Gun Club. The contractor would also make a new taxiway connection from the control tower to the hardstands, which would take away the old taxiway section that extended around the ends of the two runways 14 and 02 it would mean a shortcut taxiway for the planes.

I suggested that while they were re-laying the new taxiway from the tower they should lay a water pipe under it so that the tower could have running water, which would avoid cutting up the new taxiway at some point in the future.

The emergency call desk 2929 at the BCE office in Building 555 was inundated with calls. Iris Fletcher was running this office with help of airmen from the BCE Squadron. All these calls were guaranteed to be actioned the day they were received, not easy if spare parts were required. Iris would eventually be responsible for the control of funding, especially for projects that the AMWD were supervising; these must not overrun their original costings unless there were unforeseen circumstances.

Close neighbours – life goes on...

A Phantom lines up over Iken church for the the Bentwaters runway. [GP]

Good Neighbours – 1960s

According to Margaret, the Clerical Officer in the Air Ministry Resident Engineer's office, we at Bentwaters were in trouble with a local farmer. The fields bordering the airfield were drilled with corn and the farmer was suggesting that rabbits from the airfield were stripping his corn bare, an ongoing problem that he had complained about previously on more than one occasion. His latest letter would be copied to the local Member of Parliament if action was not taken soon, he said. Any action taken would involve funding from the Government Estates Department or the USAF. It was by no means certain that the rabbits that were eating the corn were indeed coming from the airfield side but installing rabbit wire along the present insubstantial boundary fence (consisting of three strands of wire on 4ft concrete posts) should get us off the hook. A much more secure 8ft boundary fence would later be installed.

At RAF Woodbridge a Self Help Army Air Force Engineer team arrived to erect what would be known as a Nose Dock Aircraft Hangar. The team would receive the support of the AMWD Sub District office at Woodbridge to hire plant in from local contractors and heavy lifting equipment from around the district. This would take the best part of a year and crane hire would be astronomical. The hangar had been dismantled in France and transported to Woodbridge base but not all the parts were suitable to refit and some of the parts were missing. It goes without saying that the Nose Dock project was a costly one.

When complete it was very rewarding for those involved in the construction to see a C130 Hercules rolled in and the doors close to fit around the fuselage, leaving the tail section out in the open air, allowing the engines to be worked on in the warm and dry. One could see the logic in having this nose dock with so many C130s using the Twin Bases. It would prove to be well used.

In 1966 Colonel Searles flew in the first F4 Phantom – an aircraft that would be operated by the 81st for the next 13 years. This was a very heavy (20 tons laden) aircraft but very fast, capable of Mach 2. They were very noisy on take-off when on full afterburners or 'reheat'. The switchover to this aircraft would mean a change of spares and ground equipment, as with any aircraft changeover. The ground crews must prepare for the maintenance of this plane months ahead of the first aircraft arriving. The Phantom would be in service with most of the nations in Europe and the RAF would fly them for many years, taking us into the 1980s.

Phil Shimmon has shared an Armed Forces Day Programme that his father-in-law, an airman who served at Bentwaters, saved all those years ago (see overleaf).

The summer of 1967 saw her Majesty the Queen and the Duke of Edinburgh arrive at Bentwaters in a turboprop Andover of the Queen's Flight. It was a great occasion, particularly for the RAF Station Commander and Wing Commander Colonel Richard Searles. Also in attendance was the Lieutenant of Suffolk the Earl of Stradbrook. Her Majesty was on her way to open the

ARMED FORCES DAY 21st MAY 1966

I am pleased and proud to welcome you to RAF Station Bentwaters, home of the 81st Tactical Fighter Wing, for our annual observance of Armed Forces Day. This is an opportunity for us to return, in some measure, the wonderful hospitality you have shown us in your country during the past 14 years. It is also an opportunity for us to pay tribute to the armed forces of NATO. Our theme for this event has carried such titles as "Power for Peace under NATO" and "Partners for Peace under NATO" in recent years. Though we have changed the title, this remains true this year and I am proud once again to have the RAF participating in the show with us for our joint efforts were duly recognised in this year's theme.

As members of NATO, our role is to contribute to the ultimate deterrent of those who would force their will upon the Free World. Here today you will see a representation of the men and equipment that comprise this deterrence and make the theme "The Unity and Common Purpose of the Armed Forces and U.S. Support of NATO."

Our program is designed to acquaint you with the 81st Wing, its men and equipment, and newly-assigned aircraft, the F-4C Phantom II.

Everything we have arranged is meant for your edification and pleasure.

I sincerely hope you enjoy our program, and that it contributes to your understanding of the RAF, NATO and USAF

DeWitt R. Sealers

Colonel USAF Commander

The 81st Tactical Fighter Wing Mission

The primary mission of the 81st Tactical Fighter Wing is to conduct special operations against aggressive forces in support of the North Atlantic Treaty Organisation (NATO)

The Chain of command: The 81st Tactical Fighter Wing is a NATO unit directly under the Third Air Force which in turn is responsible to the USAF in Europe (USAFE). USAFE is a major command of the USAF.

Its Bases: RAF Bentwaters and RAF Woodbridge.

Its Key People:
Wing Commander – Colonel De Witt R. Sealers
Wing Vice Commander – Colonel R. Melton
Base Commander – Colonel W. Parramore.
Deputy Commander Operations – Colonel D. Allen
Deputy Commander Material – Colonel H. Cowan

Its Aircraft: The McDonnell F-4C Phantom II

The Phantom is the U.S. Air Force 's newest, fastest, slowest, and highest flying operational jet fighter aircraft. A holder of 15 world speed records, it can be airborne in less than 3000ft runway, streak to a target at 1,600mph or fly comfortably at extremely slow speeds for a jet (125mph) in order to make short field landings safe and practical. Its two man crew has been proved operationally 30% better detection and lock-on ranges than a single man crew and its twin engines make it 60% safer than single engine fighters. In fact, should the need arise the J-79 engines are powerful enough to allow the F-4c to take a wave-off on one engine without using afterburner.

The Phantom can carry a weapons load twice that of a World War 2 bomber. It can be loaded with 18 750-pound bombs, Four infrared guided Sidewinder missile, 15 680-pound mines, four air-to-ground Bull-pup missiles, 15 air-to-ground multiple rocket packages, three 20mm Vulcan gun pods (each with a 6,000 round-per-minute rate of fire) or combination of these up to 16,000 pound local. The electronic vision of this aircraft is the keenest yet developed for it operates the largest fighter radar antenna in the free world and has repeatedly detected incoming bomber targets at extreme ranges.

ARMED FORCES DAY PROGRAM

10.00 Open Day begins. The following facilities will be open until 2pm.

Exhibit Area "A"

a. Base Cinema – Featuring The Air Force Story
b. Hobby Shops
c. Gymnasium
d. Bowling Alley
e. Library
f. Chapel
g. Recreation Centre
h. Education Centre
i. School Classroom

Exhibit Area "B"

Main Display Hangar will remain open until 5.00pm with the following exhibits.

a. F-4C Phantom II
b. Information News stand
c. b. Aero Club
d. Jet Engine Display
e. Stock Car Display
f. Survival Equipment
g. 78th Tactical Fighter Squadron
h. Cub Scout Display
i. 91st Tactical Fighter Squadron
j. Armament Display
k. 92nd Tactical Fighter Squadron
l. Munitions/Ordinance
m. Aircraft Support Equipment
n. Air Police Display
o. Parachute Packing Display
p. Rod and Gun Display
q. Weather detachment Display
r. Communication Display
s. Fire Department Display
t. Data Processing Machine

The 'Facsimile Field Hospital' would be located adjacent to the main Display Hangar (Area B); Food Sales Stand Operated by AYA, Boy and Girl Scouts, NCO and Officers Wives Clubs, Consolidated in tent equipped with tables and chairs (Area B)

USAF Aircraft on static display:

a) F-4C Phantom
b) F-100 Super Sabre
c) T-39
d) T33
e) C-47 Dakota

RAF Aircraft on static display:

f) Shackleton
g) Jet Provost
h) Gnat
i) Lightning
j) Argosy.

Air Show – Special Activities

11.00hrs Little League Ball Game Exhibition

11.30 Medieval Archery Society Demonstration

12.00 Fire Fighting Demonstration

12.30 Radio controlled Model Airplane demonstration.

1.00 Medieval Archery Society Demonstration.

1.30 Radio Controlled Model Aircraft Demonstration.

2.15 Distinguished Guests seated for Air show.

2.25 Raising of Colours and Playing of National Anthems.

2.30 Air Show begins.

2.30 "V" Bomber Fly-by touch and go demonstration

2.37 Shackleton Fly-by touch and go demonstration

2.47 F-100 4-ship Fly-by and Solo Demonstration

2.55 Helicopter Search and Rescue Demonstration

3.05 Jet Provost Solo Demonstration.

3.15 Argosy Falcons Parachute Team Drop

3.20 Lightning Solo Demonstration

3.25 F-4Cs Launch Aircraft

3.35 Argosy landing to pick up Falcons

3.38 Gnat (Red Arrows) 7-Ship Demonstration.

3.55 F-4Cs 4x4 and 16-ship fly-by (solo)

4.10 F4Cs Land

5.00 pm Armed Forces Day Activities Concluded

Snape Maltings Concert Hall in support of the composer Sir Benjamin Britten.

There was some scepticism by a few of the one thousand British Workers employed at Bentwaters, who thought this important visit by Her Majesty spelt the beginning of the end to their employment here, the rundown of the military base and the end of all flying in due course. There would be pressure from the concert hall, should there ever be a reduction in the number of NATO airfields required, for Bentwaters to be one of the first to fall. Time would tell...

During his time as commander Colonel Searles was invited to attend the 50 year celebration of the opening of RAF Martlesham Heath on 16th January 1967, where he laid a wreath on the war memorial situated on the old barrack square. Richard Searles had served in the WW2 European campaign as a young fighter pilot.

We have reached July 1967 and another change of command for the 81st as Colonel Ramon Melton assumed command for the next year. Colonel Searles took promotion to Brigadier General back in the USA, where an office job awaited. A number of ex-Bentwaters Wing Commanders were promoted to Brigadier General as they departed the old base.

Without a doubt Bentwaters was a challenge like no other: a lot of work, skilled planning and fierce competition for funds was called for if the base was ever to be brought up to a Class 'A' NATO Establishment.

In September 1967 there was a jet aircraft crash at the west end of the Bentwaters base when an F4c was totally wrecked in the fir trees, a severe blow to the 81st Operations Squadron. The F4c had been in operational service here for only a few months. Without a doubt, a full investigation would follow.

The long-awaited perimeter road leading from the Rod & Gun Club to Building 172 (the Ground Power Shop) near the church was finally underway and expected to be in use by

all the traffic heading for the other side of the airfield in a few weeks. This was great news – no more hold-ups at the traffic lights and no more claims by the contractors for time lost awaiting a green light.

There was a huge oil trap at the lowest end to deal with any oil spillage before rainwater was discharged into the river at Butley Creek. The landing light poles extended way beyond it across the neighbouring farmer's field.

The base was getting funds for urgent projects but the word going round was that should the USAF be at Bentwaters for 20 years the reconstruction of the base would be about half complete!

Wartime Bentwaters had a small cinema on the communal site adjacent the NAAFI but this was demolished to make way for a beer store. So there was an urgent need for a cinema/theatre and the site chosen was opposite the Chapel. This theatre would be a 400+ seater and the seats would be spaced for everyone to enjoy the comfort of plenty of legroom. The Americans liked plenty of space. Sadler would construct the very modern building, which would have a sloping floor back to front as all theatres do. The stage would be particularly large and spacious with changing rooms, etc, where stage stars would perform to entertain the troops.

Construction was progressing and steel columns were built into the brickwork ready to take the roof but, with the steelwork at roof level, an error was discovered. The theatre was two feet lower in the ground than the survey drawings were showing. Oh dear! The site agent for Sadler was in complete shock and a top level meeting between all parties was arranged. After going through the entire measuring procedure and a debate on how best to get around this major error it was decided that the contractor would weld 2-foot extension pieces to the steel columns and complete the roof at the required level. A most unfortunate situation and, needless to say, the site agent was not happy for some time afterwards. Supervising staff at all levels

The Avro Vulcan 'V' Bomber was another favourite with the show crowd.

in all departments, including AMWD, did not get away without a roasting from their bosses.

During the demolition of all the Base facilities to make way for the new Housing Development (Rendlesham Park) in 2003 the theatre was the last building to be removed. It was sad to see it go.

The new FC4 Phantom aircraft were all in place with the three squadrons and were taking up operational duties to serve NATO. BCE Staff would be heavily involved in the installation of the new arrestor barrier to be known as the BAK9. This was a steel cable that lay across the runway awaiting a hook on the aircraft to engage and bring the aircraft to a rapid halt, similar to the system used on aircraft carriers. The cable was on a drum beside the runway underground in a reinforced concrete pit with an access ladder and working space for general maintenance. These barriers would be at both ends of the 08-26 runway, suspended on 'doughnuts', as they were known, to keep the cable 4 inches above the runway surface so that the hook could correctly engage for a perfect stop. The doughnuts were rubber discs about 10ins in diameter and a half inch thick with the cable

passing through the centre, evenly spaced at approximately 2 feet apart to support the cable over the 50 yard wide runway.

Although the Phantom was fitted with drogue chute braking, the arrestor cable was essential should there be a failure at any time.

The main 08-26 runway had to be over-slabbed again. It was over 10 years since any major work had been done, which meant the aircraft had to be relocated to Woodbridge and the forward bases for several weeks. This over-slab work to the main runway was performed on four occasions at Bentwaters, which added to the original 8 inch pavement quality concrete on 4 inch rolled dry-lean to make the overall thickness of the runway over 42 inches. Over-slabbing the runway always gave an opportunity for other work to be carried out which had not been possible because of the flying activities over the past 10 years; such as major maintenance on airfield lighting, the MA1A Barrier, overrun areas and runway drainage pits, etc.

I have not mentioned the Communications set-up at Bentwaters and RAF Martlesham Heath – the ROC as it was known – located on the Foxhall-Ipswich road and a very active unit very much in touch with Fylingdale, the early warning satellite station and in support of the surrounding bases. We would give this off-base facility all the support necessary to maintain its effectiveness. It had an electrical supply backup generator that was manned around the clock by our diesel generator shift engineers. On one occasion portable generators were brought on site to supply power around the clock to a section of the equipment for several days, to the displeasure of the residents of Bell Lane, Kesgrave. The local council asked the military to take action to ease the problem, which they attempted to do, with the aid of bales of straw stacked high around the generators – until sparks from the generators did the inevitable. Thankfully the Fire Department was soon on site to get the fire under control without any damage to the valuable equipment and soon afterwards the emergency work was completed and the generators could be switched off, bringing peace back to the area.

The Communications Service, like the Bentwaters Support Squadrons, gave support to the four forward bases in Germany. These bases were used as training locations by the Squadron aircraft and the BCE Squadron. Personnel which included the project funding section Mrs Iris Fletcher and her financial wiz-kids were expected to visit these locations and apply for the necessary funding, all as part of the rebuild and refurbishing for the benefit of the 81st FBW supporting NATO. Great Bromley in Essex was another Communications site that the USAF found necessary for their operations.

And the Bentwaters telephone switchboard was about to go automatic!

The Queen drops in at Bentwaters en route to the official opening of the Snape Maltings Concert Hall. [EADT]

We Progress into the 1970s

As well as all the military-funded facilities at the Twin Bases, a number of additional recreational and social facilities were sustained by what was known as Non Appropriated Funds (NAF). The American Open Clubs, as they were known, were non-military when it came to funding. Top Four Club and the Officers Club were just two of the many small units that came under the heading of NAF. These clubs made their own money as they went along, providing eating facilities and entertainment, snooker tables, bars and slot machines. A separate accounts office for all these clubs within NAF was run by Wilfred Robst, who had been working at Bentwaters in the warehouse office. He employed his own staff to keep on top of the workload. Wilf was German and had been detained here as a prisoner of war but when the time came for him to go back to Germany, Wilf felt sure that he could make it here in good old England and chose to stay.

The Top Four Club had been extended but during shutdown retained their assistant manager, Mr Karol from Poland. A chap called Stan was a barman and a lady named Gladys was a waitress in the Officers Club.

The Child Care Centre was another ongoing and profitable organisation that had picked up well since it began just before the married quarters were occupied. This facility was relocated to provide more space to meet the needs of growing families. Mrs Jean Friend ran the Child Care Centre for many years.

The sports fields on both bases were now heavily in use. Ivy Lodge Gate was an area where baseball was played and American-style 'bleachers' (tiered seating) was set up to provide spectators with a relaxing view.

Bentwaters lacked sufficient space for all those who wished to participate in the various sporting activities on offer and it became clear that more space would have to be obtained to meet the demand. Woodbridge, on the other hand, had a large football pitch with bleachers around the entire field, where the 81st Wing American Football Team could play matches

The former Open Mess 'Top Four Club' at Bentwaters. [MH]

against other Wing teams, with the odd drink/candy/hotdog stall thrown in.

Volleyball was popular and the teams from Bentwaters were successful (see panel).

Leagues and knockout competitions in other American sports such as baseball and basketball were organised hotly contested between teams from the many USAF bases in Europe.

Indoor bowling was very well supported and this popular facility at Bentwaters, with its many bowling lanes, was heavily used by all members of the family.

The High School at Woodbridge Base was becoming a reality with the first set of classrooms erected. More would need to be planned and built to accommodate the number of children arriving as families took up all 68 Bentwaters and 248 Woodbridge married quarters, together with off-base private dwellings wherever they could be found.

I must just tell you of a visit I made to the 91st Squadron Operations building and their coffee bar, where an attractive blonde lady and her young daughter were busy but also wrestling with leaky cold water tap, which had brought me on the scene, accompanied by a plumber to correct the offender. While we were there an officer pilot approached the bar and purchased a coffee for the sum of whatever but he had to pay in English money and wrestled the old problem. He was very confused with this '12 pence equals 1 shilling' and '240 pence equals 1 pound' and was anxious to know when we were going to round things up and become decimal in this great little country of ours? A few years later, we made it at last.

In 1968 Colonel Melton the 81st Wing Commander for the past year was moving on and the Wing would be commanded by Colonel George S. Dorman. Records show that Colonel Dorman and Colonel Devol Brett were both in command of the Wing for a period during 1968.

Colonel Dorman served as Wing Commander during the summer of that year and was then posted to Vietnam. It is not clear how long he was on active service in war-torn Vietnam but sadly Colonel George S. Dorman was killed in action while serving with the USAF Far East. It was a shock to everyone in the 81st FBW and a memorial was to be set up in the colonel's memory. An engraved marble archway was ordered and erected at the entrance to the Woodbridge Football Field. Everyone admired the flowers as they passed through to enjoy the game.

Colonel Devol Brett was another Wing Commander who served the 81st Wing until Summer 1969. Colonel Brett would be remembered for his drum kit. He was very good at playing the drums and with his Austrian wife able to play the piano, you had the perfect pair to entertain the guests. Once again my wife Lottie and Dick the cook from the Officers Mess were busy in the big bungalow kitchen arranging the delights for the evening.

Now back at the workplace at Woodbridge the 20th TFW 79th Squadron had announced that they were pulling out of Woodbridge as an operational force and returning to Upper Heyford, the 20th HQ.

So the F-100s were leaving too and locals would miss the single-engine fighters of the 79th that had occupied the skies over and around Woodbridge town for the past 14 years.

The 79th had moved into the Suffolk base in 1955, of which was meant to be only a short temporary move but lasted all those years and in that time a lot of friends were made. Former 81st Wing personnel who served at Woodbridge will tell you that some of the 79th and 78th people were maintaining their friendships well into the 21st century.

With the 79th leaving it would mean that the 78th Squadron would have much more room and more facilities at their disposal – or would it?? The authorities may have other operational needs to fit into the Woodbridge base.

Bentwaters had another Phantom aircraft accident. During a two-ship take-off in a westerly direction, one aircraft ran into trouble soon after it left the airfield boundary and the pilot was desperate to return to base. He suggested to the control tower that he return to base, landing downwind to get down as quickly as he can, and was given the go-ahead to do so.

The Phantom proved to be a noisy aircraft not to everybody's liking. [GP]

Model shows how the local haulier brought the bird home from the carrot field.

Unfortunately, he didn't touch down as early as he should have and with only half the runway length to brake and stop, the aircraft would ran out of landing surface and entered the overrun area.

The BAK9 barrier was not engaged at the take-off end so the MA1A barrier was quickly deployed from the control tower but this was ineffective with a plane travelling at such a speed. Only the base boundary fence and the landing light poles would slow the F-4C down as it came to rest in the adjoining carrot field. I remember one of the pilots getting out of the aircraft and retreating back over the broken fence and walking up the sharp incline away from the wreckage. A civilian oil tanker driver Mr Drewery proceeded towards the wrecked aircraft to try and help the second pilot out but the 1st pilot told him not to go near the aircraft and leave everything; everyone was told to keep well back in case of fire.

It was mid-morning and all aircraft were diverted to Woodbridge. It was some time before the decision to remove the wreck was taken and it was nightfall before the 50-ton electric crane arrived from the Woodbridge base. This crane was huge, the wheels were 8ft in diameter and under normal circumstances would lift this bird and relocate it to wherever it needed to go. The number of people involved was substantial and it was apparent to the chief in charge that when the aircraft

was lifted off the ground and the crane moved out of the field, the rough terrain would cause the aircraft to swing, so ropes were attached at the four points of the aircraft and as many as four or five airmen on each rope were to told to hold the plane from side movement. Unfortunately the terrain was too rough and neither the men nor the crane were able to control the swinging aircraft, which fell to the ground with the crane then toppling on top of it. It was too late to retrieve the wreck tonight; the air police would have to watch things until daybreak.

I turned up the next morning to arrange with a contractor to get the fence replaced and made secure and to my surprise I discovered that Pickfords, the local hauliers, had been on site since daybreak and had retrieved the crane, which was already on its way back to Woodbridge base, and loaded the Phantom onto a flat bed. The crane only travelled at 7mph, so it would be a while before it reached Woodbridge motor pool.

Pickfords were tracking along the runway with the Phantom, heading for the investigation area and the aircraft's final resting place. This had been an unfortunate accident but fortunately had been contained within the environs of the base boundary, which the USAF Commanders would be grateful for and with only slight injuries to the aircrew, who would be back in the air again before too long.

Following the F4C carrot field accident at Bentwaters, when had the BAK9 cable had been in place on the morning of the accident the aircraft could have been saved, an order was issued that from now on both the BAK9 barriers on the Twin Bases would be engaged at both the landing and take-off ends of the main runways at all times. However, this full time engagement of the BAK9 would mean additional wear and tear to the surface immediately underneath the steel cable. The reason I raise this point is because we already had noted excessive wear under the cable at the far end where the aircraft ran over it before clearing the runway.

We were forever calling on the specialist runway contractors at London Heath Row to work at the weekend to cut out and replace a two-foot wide concrete strip under the cable using a special expensive epoxy-resin rapid hardener. These specialist contractors had a full-time job at Heath Row and were not always available. In due course a second set of barriers would be installed further up the runway.

One particular weekend when the contractors had to repair a storm drain and the pit cover just off the edge of the east end runway, it was just before 3pm on Sunday afternoon when we were warned that an F4c Phantom would be taking off imminently. If he was not airborne by 3pm he could not go (due to a local agreement regarding church services). It was dead on three o'clock when the aircraft taxied past and turned, taking off very quickly ad giving us an unexpected full blast from his twin engines. This blew away our temporary portable shelter, which struck a workman, resulting in blood streaming from a head wound. This unsatisfactory state of affairs was reported to the tower, who said they would report the incident to the pilot's base in Germany. Apparently he had experienced engine starting problems, which delayed him from taking to the air at 2.55pm as planned.

In August 1969 Colonel David J. Schmerbeck would take over as Wing Commander until March 1970. Colonel Schmerbeck would see the conversion of the Woodbridge 78th Squadron F4Cs to F4Ds. Conversion of the Bentwaters Phantoms with the 91st and 92nd would follow later.

This was a particularly special time for me since I had applied for promotion myself and accepted a posting to Orfordness as a Technical Officer Grade 4, a junior post that I wanted, on the American project called *Cobra Mist* working for the Radio Corporation of America (RCA). I would be at Orfordness for six months, during which time pile driving was ongoing to create foundations for the Arial Masts. Hollow steel tubes 12ins in diameter were driven to well over 100ft deep before being filled with dry-lean concrete to

The BAK9 barrier at Bentwaters. [NR]

support the concrete base which would take the antenna. I then moved to Mahe in the Seychelles for six months. The project here was to construct an airfield on the seashore. The runway would be a 14in-thick concrete slab on 4 inches of dry-lean foundation; 9,000 feet long by 50 yards wide to take the largest of holiday jet airliners.

Most of the work was already 50% complete; I was replacing a quality control officer returning home on compassionate grounds. So from working at Orfordness Island, six miles from home, I found myself in Mahe, capital of the Seychelles, six thousand miles from home. Before I returned to the UK in March 1971 I witnessed a C130 RAF aircraft land on the new runway which had come over from RAF Gan.

I had been kept up to date with the goings-on at the Twin Bases during my absence and would soon see what a difference a year had made. Woodbridge, I noticed, was now being used not just by the 78th Squadron but also by the 67th (ARRS) Aerospace Rescue Recovery Squadron. This was a very good move. They had come up from the Spanish region and would be covering a very large area of the southern hemisphere for all types of rescue work. They operated the Jolly Green Giant Helicopter as well as the C130.

We can see now the purpose for the Nose Dock that completed last year for the maintenance of C130s.

The 67th would make use of the wide open spaces of Sutton Heath adjoining the Woodbridge base for their rescue practices.

Woodbridge base was used extensively during the 1960s and 1970s for Wing football games and many other open events. Large crowds gathered and use the bleachers around the perimeter to watch the Red Arrows RAF display team. A number of British local girls were there to enjoy a day out with their American boyfriends, and why not? The GI lads and off duty aircrew were all into American Football.

'Miss Anglia' Nanette Slack, who later became a senior officer's wife. [EADT]

One particular Ipswich young lady in attendance with her girlfriends and boyfriends was Nanette Slack, who was something special in the beauty contest world. Beginning in the mid-1960s she won over 200 beauty titles in her heyday among them she was voted Ocean Princess at Southampton, Miss Anglia, Miss TV Times, Miss Ipswich Town and Miss Norwich. When she won the big prize and became Butlins Holiday Princess she walked straight into Mann Edgerton's in Ipswich and bought a Vauxhall Viva for her Dad. What a lovely thought. She was recognised particularly here at Woodbridge base with her jet pilot boyfriend William Olsen. He hoped to marry Nanette very soon. He was in no doubt that he would rise through the ranks to become a colonel one day, travelling wherever the air force took him. After a whirlwind courtship they were married in the 70s and were certain to return to the UK one day.

I returned to the UK in 1971 after my short tour of duty in the Seychelles, where I had seen the completion of the airport for the rich and famous to enjoy a sunshine snorkelling holiday to admire the colourful and amazing sea life. As the lads told me, as you yourself get darker skinned the females seem to look whiter – "funny thing, Nature."

While I was at Mahe the Government Department that I serve changed its name to the Department of Environment (DoE). It seemed like only a short time ago that the Air Ministry Works Department (AMWD) was changed to the Ministry of Public Building & Works (MPBW). Perhaps we could expect another change in a year or so.

During 1970 Colonel John C. Bartholf was Wing Commander from March to September and on my return in March Colonel James W. Enos was the Wing Commander from Sept 1970 until June 1971.

For some time now there had been a Station Maintenance and Repair Team (SMART) consisting of a group of tradesmen: a plumber, a carpenter, a painter & decorator and an electrician working from a mobile workshop equipped with all the tools and materials they needed to effect repairs to the buildings. These tradesmen set up shop and spent about a week on site, leaving the buildings in a reasonable state of repair until they returned, having completed a full circuit of the base. This practice was necessary for the upkeep of old tin hut accommodation still used for the Hospital, Headquarters Buildings and Site 4 Single Officers' Quarters and it proved very satisfactory.

It was not surprising that some of the young single pilots had moved off base out of the tin huts on Site 4 to share as a group in large country dwellings offering decent accommodation and giving them independence, although they had to fend for themselves. They were quite content to do the cooking, washing dishes and general duties in return for enjoying off-base living.

Colonel Dwaine L. Weatherwax took the Wing Commander's job for the next year, taking us to August.

In 1972 one of the Colonel's duties included bidding happy retirement to my friend Chief Sergeant Mason Hire, with all the decorations that entailed. Mason, you will remember, came to Bentwaters in the late 1960s and settled down with his family at Wickham Market, where he still lives today (2004). After leaving the service, Mason took a civilian job at the Base newsstand for many years and now lives alone (his dear wife died last year) in the bungalow adjacent Wickham Market School.

I returned to the fold to assume the duties of Quality Control Officer for a new project: "Maintenance Control Facilities" costing $1 million to be constructed by R.G. Carter of Great Yarmouth. Most of the workforce would travel from Lowestoft night and morning, in excess of a 70-mile round trip. This project would benefit the Squadron personnel enormously, providing single-storey workshops and a two-storey Maintenance Control Building for the office staff with computer control to identify each individual aircraft.

Included in this project was a sewage pump house construction intended to discharge sewage from the south side of the airfield to the main sewage disposal works two miles away at Rendlesham Park. It meant that we had to cross the main runway by means of drawing the new 6-inch pipes through the existing duct laid under the runway before resurfacing in the mid-1960s. Pumping the sewage to the main sewage works direct would be a big money saver, cancelling all those tanker loads that had to be contracted out on a daily and weekly basis.

I mentioned some time ago that pressure was on to find more housing and more sports field area, mainly at Bentwaters. At Bury Hill, Woodbridge, there was a housing estate that was now ready for occupation to rent and many of the American families who were seeking accommodation moved into this estate by arrangement with the USAF authorities via a lease agreement. Bury Hill was situated at the top of Woods Lane, Melton, Woodbridge.

It's was in the early 1970s that W.C. French contractors moved onto Rendlesham Park to construct 300 MFH for the USAF families on a 10-year lease. This area was adjacent to the base but not part of the Air Ministry owned land. The only connection the Ministry had with this parkland was that the sewage pipe for the whole base ran across the entire park, leading to the sewage works. This stinking wartime pump house with its open well would now be built around with 2-storey flats and 2/3 bedroom houses. This Housing project would go some way to meeting the urgent accommodation for the USAF families.

In the meantime there was a major improvement of both Bentwaters and Woodbridge Weapons Dumps where security was improved by installing a double fence topped with razor wire for safer and better patrolling. New Gate Houses and electric emergency power generators were also installed with electric powered personnel and vehicle gates.

The 1970s brought additional responsibilities as anti-shipping missions and other duties were given to the Wing but the F-4C and F-4D Phantom II fighters coped well. Pilots also began training with U.S. Army ground controllers in central Europe, beginning the backdrop for the wing's future as a close air support unit for NATO.

The Bentwaters Control tower got a facelift with sun deflectors and air conditioning to ease the high temperatures in the top controller's cabin.

Monday 21st August 1972 was a sad day when we experienced a mid-air collision between two Bentwaters Phantoms. The two aircraft collide over the sea seven miles out from Lowestoft with the loss of one of the aircraft. One Phantom, piloted by Captain Scheck with his navigator Major Chittenden managed to return to Bentwaters base and land safely. The other F-4c went down in the sea with the loss of both airmen. It was remarkable that Captain Scheck landed the damaged aircraft with a large section of the tail missing. A USAF spokesman stated that "he did a damned good job landing it." This collision came just at the time when there was

The Bentwaters Control Tower with its new air-conditioned top cabin.

Phantom showing damage after a mid-air collision over the North Sea. [USAF]

a change of Wing Commanders as Colonel Dwaine Weatherwax handed over to Colonel Charles Word.

Colonel Charles E. Word took the Wing Commander's slot from August 1972 to April 1974. The conversion of F-4C to F-4D was complete and Colonel Word would have the pleasure of seeing Wing personnel move into new facilities that had been designed, funded and constructed as a result of hard work by everyone, particularly the BCE planning and finance sections.

Everything was gathering momentum after 20 years. Each section or squadron now knew what was required of them to be a complete successful operating Wing. At Bentwaters large warehouses had been constructed, the motor pool was extended and the 91st Squadron had moved from Building 59 (the large tin hut complex) to the south side of the airfield. Building 59 would now be a temporary mail collection point. This wall of steel lockers was a sight to be seen as every individual or family was given a collection point number to make their daily call. We need a new Post Office!

The new Maintenance Control facilities were near completion and I would be moving to Woodbridge base to take up a post (with some help) covering the maintenance of all the facilities including the supervising of airfield grass maintenance contractors. The 'bird grass' as we called it at Bentwaters was left at 8 inches high to serve as a bird deterrent adjacent to the main runway but this did not apply at Woodbridge because we had a very wide runway with outer strips (known as 'infield' and 'outfield').

The High School at Woodbridge was increasing in size and more and more teenagers were signing up to attend. The school buses were increasing in numbers and providing play areas for this mass of young people was proving difficult. The base gym at Woodbridge was used by the service personnel and the school on a shared basis, not an ideal arrangement but the promised new School Gym is still a long way off.

The Chapel at Woodbridge had been constructed at the same time as the early Married Family Housing and was nicely established with its own garden, blending in with the old established fir trees. The redecoration of MFH was a continuous ongoing job for two or sometimes three painters. As families moved out and returned to the States each vacant MFH had to be checked for repairs and repainted. Woodbridge had over 250 housing units which rotated continuously.

The schools were also very demanding as far as maintenance went and planning with the contractor was essential, particularly during summer holidays.

These Twin Bases were very similar to a small town with all their supporting amenities and the BCE and Ministry staff were aware that they were not just dealing with a temporary air force base.

The Twin Bases had their own high voltage distribution centres, water supply and treatment plant, sewage disposal works and every type of user facility, such as Cinema/Theatre, Restaurants, Shops, Hair Dressers, Bowling Alley, News Stand, Laundromat and there was more programmed, calling for a very complex and demanding mixture of specialised skills and trades.

And we were still only about half way through the reconstruction of the Twin Bases to make the 81st Wing a 1st class NATO base.

As has been mentioned there was evidence that many of the USAF personnel were not leaving the twin bases to explore the English countryside. The facilities on base were sufficient and generally me their needs.

The 3 Phantom Squadrons were operating to full capacity serving NATO night and day training to meet any challenge facing the Fighter Tactical Wing.

The F-4Ds, like the F-4Cs had very noisy engines and the testing of these at the engine testing bay was creating hell. Testing was necessary after the unit had been overhauled. There had been different steel defectors installed but these didn't provide any benefit as regards lowering the noise level so it was decided that when under test these engines must be enclosed and suppressed by the 'water tunnel method'. This was a very costly project but we must be seen to make every effort to give our near neighbours some relief from this ear busting racket. Once installed the steam from the suppressor could be seen for miles around but without a sound. Well done!

Colonel John R. Paulk took over as Wing Commander from April 1974 to May 1975. I had the pleasure of meeting the Colonel one morning during the summer of 1974 when he had called a meeting at the Woodbridge sports field for a number of high-ranking officers and we 'men from the Ministry'. It concerned the bad state of the football field.

The Colonel had received complaints from football team members and something had to be sorted out. John Paulk asked why the finished grass surface was in such poor condition and could things be improved in the next few days for the forthcoming match? I said it was difficult to maintain a good playing surface while the area was over played by the school children. The grass area needed to be rested between matches. The very light soil and poor grass in this area did not stand up to continuous heavy use. It was difficult to say when the football field could be reinstated or the grass re-grow to form a suitable surface.

The Colonel took the Base Commander to one side (the Base Commander was answerable for the school activities). I would imagine his orders were to try to keep the children off but this could prove difficult, especially out of school hours.

It was about this time that Bentwaters had a 'power outage' – an expression the Americans used when the electrical power failed. The reason for the failure was not clear, all the fuses and switchgear controls had been checked and now cables to the incoming substation would have to be checked also.

The old half mile road had been closed since the new bypass was opened in the early

1960s and this was where the cable feeding Bentwaters Base from the Eastern Electricity main supply crossed the old road to the substation – and this was where the problem was discovered. Mr Bob Meadows, a keen rabbit catcher, had been anxious to retrieve his ferret, which was under ground in a rabbit burrow and required digging out to free the ferret's leash, which was presumably snagged around a tree root, or so he thought. But instead of a root it was a high tension cable that he severed.

Bob was using a long wooden-handled 'spoon', as they were known in the trade. He was blinded by the flash for a few seconds, not to mention a little shocked, but was otherwise unharmed. He remarked that it did appear to be 'rather a tough root'. A lucky man.

The Married Quarters at RAF Martlesham Heath had been offered to the USAF Twin Bases to help them out with their housing shortage problem; the offer wouldn't entirely solve the problem but would certainly help. There were over 30 MFH at Hilton Road, Martlesham and 12 at Portal Avenue. These needed some attention to the heating, plumbing and electrical wiring, but attention they would get, so that families could move in as soon as possible.

In Hilton Road the twin quarters were named after familiar aircraft such as Lancaster and Halifax, and the names of the roads Anson, "B" Flight Road and others similar. Portal Avenue (there was an Air Chief Marshal, later Lord Portal) was an up-market housing area where the RAF Station Commander and other high ranking officers lived in 4-bedroom houses with spacious gardens. One of these gardens contained a high mound of soil topped with grass that should not be disturbed because, we were informed, it was to remain a burial site. There was a file in the office relating to this.

Single officer's accommodation continued to be in short supply, mainly due to so many visiting officers on short visits. 30 housing units were refurbished to accommodate single officers and this did help a desperate situation. Ministry of Defence housing units

The Base Theatre, a much used and appreciated facility, was demolished in 2003.

at Shotley, Felixstowe and Ipswich were also offered to the Americans of the 81st Wing.

It was now May 1975 and Colonel Clyde H. Garner was the Wing Commander for the next 9 months. I had the pleasure of meeting Colonel Garner at a progress meeting one Wednesday morning. Weekly progress meetings were ongoing. He expressed concern for the general wellbeing of everyone on the Bury Hill estate saying that he would have to get the families off Bury Hill and that it was quite unacceptable for families to be there. There was no space for children to exercise and life was being made difficult for everyone in these cramped conditions. Eventually the Bury Hill estate was vacated by the American families, who were accommodated mainly in the Rendlesham Park complex.

I have mentioned 20 Colonels so far who had served as Wing Commanders at Bentwaters since the 81st TFW arrived in 1951 up to February 1976. Most of them departed Bentwaters on promotion, giving some indication of how hard everyone has worked towards making this Wing one of the most successful in NATO.

Providing a quick response to families who had a domestic emergency such as a power outage or a plumbing problem in their married quarter was proving to be a challenge.

In order to provide a faster service the DOE set up a Do it Now (DIN) truck system. Mobile workmen in trucks were radio controlled by a central desk to provide customer support throughout the working day. Electricians working in shifts would operate around the clock and should the power fail at any time backup generators would take over at all important venues. You will recall that during the war years Bentwaters had only the one generator (our Mr Hicks worked to get it to perfection) to supply the airfield and Hospital. Small generators were now more plentiful.

The DIN truck was one of the most successful ideas (service when you want it) but, of course, came at a cost. I remember Mr Wiseman on the Bentwaters (DIN) truck and at Woodbridge we had Mr Walter Barodka, originally from Poland. Walter received his long service certificate, as was customary for civil servants, after 25 years of service.

The 21st Wing Commander at the Twin bases was Colonel Gerald D. Larson who would be in command for 15 months.

Every July 4th we expected the Americans to celebrate Independence Day but 1976 was a special year, the bicentennial marking 200 years since our Yankee cousins gained their independence from Britain so the celebrations

The PSA Group, Manager presents Walter Barodka with a Long Service Certificate celebrating 25 years employment at the Base.

would be something special. We would see a mass of vehicles heading towards the control tower and soon it was evident that a fairground had been arranged for the families to enjoy the joy rides, dodgems, steam horses, and all the fun of the fair. It was going to be a long day and the children would make the most of it.

The 81st had been at Bentwaters for 25 years and after spending much time and money they had provided employment and created a comfortable and smart looking base from an old wartime station that was all but finished.

We now move on to 1977 and I was off to supervise work at Mildenhall for the next few months, where W.C. French were erecting what I called the C130 Hangars and a Hangar named Pile Hangar (so called after the design engineer) which would completely accommodate a C141 Starlifter.

Nose Dock / Maintenance Hangar for the C130 at RAF Woodbridge. [USAF]

The C130, workhorse of 67th Rescue Squadron. [GP]

The Ivy Lodge Gate at Bentwaters was a picturesque historic feature.

The former Base Exchange building, once a hive of activity, awaits demolition.

More Developments into the 1980s

It was all very interesting at Mildenhall but I returned to work at the Twin Bases in September 1977 with the Ministry team to start the construction of the new Aircraft Shelters. The new Wing Commander for the next two years was Colonel Rudolph F. Wacker, who would see his Twin Bases flight line areas turned into a building site during the largest and most expensive Aircraft Shelter Construction project ever undertaken.

Costain Construction moved into both bases and set up office accommodation that would have to stand up to many months of heavy use by the 100 men or so who would change the face of the Twin Bases forever. (Costain had been the contractors in the Seychelles during my sojourn there, so I met up with some old friends again.)

Colonel Wacker was very involved in everything that was going on, as all Wing Commanders were, but in particular Rudolph Wacker was pushing for "space for sports" and making enquiries outside the base to hire a field that would provide the answer to an ongoing problem at Bentwaters – more space for the boys.

A local farmer, Captain Robin Sheepshanks, who owned most of the land around the domestic part of the base, agreed to let a field adjacent to the Commissary and extending up to the roundabout on the Bentwaters by-pass for USAF sports activities. The Ministry were to advise on the cultivation and grass seeding and the (BCE) Squadron would maintain the area and do the necessary marking out for various sports. This was a wonderful move on the part of the Colonel and would prove to be an asset for some time in the future.

There was a slight problem keeping the foot traffic off while the grass grew because 'the troops' (as we called all military personnel) were taking a shortcut straight across the field to the Commissary from the roundabout. Roping off the field helped a little to protect the grass but there were still the odd one or two who didn't want to walk the long way around so an authorized path was constructed by the boys from the BCE Squadron to spare the grass. The beginning of this path was indicated by a concrete slab with their names carved into it inset in the grassed area adjacent to the roundabout.

The Shelter Project was proving slow to get off the ground. I would be taking the Part I Shelter project as the Ministry Man over at Woodbridge and was given my own Portakabin office. One of the most important things to keep an eye on was the possibility of Foreign Object Damage from all the mud in particular that goes with any construction site. Contractors would be briefed to give way at all times to taxiing aircraft and to observe all traffic control signals.

It was expected that 12 or more shelters would be constructed at Woodbridge and double that number at Bentwaters. The shelters were to be constructed in the shape of the familiar Nissan hut, the steel lining to act as the internal shuttering remaining in place providing the inside galvanised finish. The steel lining would be covered in reinforced concrete 2ft thick, resting on a 3ft wide foundation. The steel framed concrete filled doors would be electrically operated, which was the only way that the doors could operate, as they weighed over 1 ton per door.

The contract period was over a year and a half and the cost would reach almost $1 million per shelter. The ministry had an on-site Senior Civil Engineer and the Project Manager and his assistant attended monthly meetings from Ruislip, London.

In spite of this mass of work going on, the Phantoms had very few problems keeping up with their operational programme. As the 1966 Open Day programme said, it was an aircraft that could be relied upon. The Phantom had been with us at the Twin Bases for 12 years and the talk was that we could expect a change at the end of the decade.

The Bulk Fuel Installations were to be increased in capacity at Bentwaters and a plan was on the cards to feed these new semi-buried fuel tanks by the National Fuel Distribution Pipeline. After the tanker drivers strike a few years previously NATO would never allow their operations to be interrupted by industrial action or any other problem with the fuel supply. By keeping a large amount of fuel in reserve at all times they could ensure that the aircraft would keep flying and that the security umbrella provided by NATO would be maintained.

As we move towards the end of the 1970s much had already been accomplished and we had seen the back of most of the wartime tin huts. But we still had more to do and a very large planning programme for the Twin Bases had been submitted to USAF HQ in Germany.

If you didn't get your bids in then you wouldn't stand any chance of getting the bucks when the funding committee met to award the end of year dollars for urgent projects. It was a crucial time as far as getting the funds for certain projects was concerned. Mrs Iris Fletcher, the BCE financial officer, was particularly good at getting the projects funded during this period. The 81st would make sure Iris was working for them until late on the last day of the financial year to bid for those remaining dollars.

Meanwhile the 67ARRS at Woodbridge were very involved in training sessions, particularly on the heathland adjacent to the weapons storage area. The Commander for 67th – Colonel M. Teed – was invited to a gathering which included the presence of Prince Charles. 'My Dad taking tea with the Prince' is something that Chad Teed, the Colonel's son, would remember from his schooldays at Woodbridge.

In 1978/9 I transferred from the Ministry of Public Buildings and Works to the Ministry of Defence on secondment to the BCE Planning Department. Colonel Kirk, who was the head of BCE in the mid-1970s, believed that I could be of great help in the planning of some projects. My boss at the beginning was Chief Master Sergeant J. Johnson (who later became Wing Sergeant Major). We all called him 'JJ'. He was a very helpful guy to me. He loved cross-country running.

I also met and worked with Sergeant Pete Cook. After these two Sergeants left the Squadron, things went downhill and I have to say that this three-year secondment was not the happiest period of my working life. But as they say, you can't win 'em all! There was one happy week that was memorable, however. Pete had a daughter who married a very nice airman and Pete and his English-born wife Margaret arranged the wedding ceremony to be held at the Base chapel. I hired the village hall at Sutton for them and arranged the wedding cars – a black Austin Princess taxi to match mine – so these two cars were bride and bridesmaids cars. I played the disco music in the evening and a good time we all had, and for me a great experience.

I remember the sad goodbyes when Margaret and Pete returned to the States. It was particularly painful for Margaret, who had her roots here in the Midlands and was a special friend of the late Iris Fletcher; I regret not keeping in touch.

Artists impression of an A-10 Thunderbolt II – also known as a 'Tankbuster'. [GP]

'Jolly Green Giant' (Sikorsky MH53m Pave Penny long-range rescue helicopter) belonging to ARRS 67th Squadron USAF on exercises at Woodbridge Weapons Dump. [GP]

In early 1979 the Twin Bases had a covering of snow and Colonel R. Wacker has flown in the first of the new aircraft to Bentwaters for the 81st Wing. This new aircraft is the A10 Thunderbolt II 'Tankbuster' with a gun so powerful it can destroy a Sherman tank. The Wing would receive up to 125 of these aircraft, which would be made up into six squadrons. In addition to the 78th, 91st, and the 92nd Squadrons 509, 510 and 511 would be flying the A10 Thunderbolt II.

The A10 was not the most glamorous aircraft to grace the skies but was a very good combat aircraft in support of field warfare. This new aircraft was so different to the F-4D Phantom. The Engine noise was totally different. Gone was the gut-wrenching sound of the Phantom; we now had a whistle sound from the A10, which I must say was a little irritating, but bearable. The new aircraft would be with us for some time to come.

It was summer and air show time again and 81st Wing agreed to include a 2-ship A10 fly-by at the Chicksands Bedfordshire Families open day. The A10 pilots for this Saturday display were Colonel Tommy Thompson, one of the most experienced A-10 pilots, and Major Glen Profitt, also a very experienced pilot with approximately 600 flown missions, mostly in Vietnam. Sadly, as Col. Thompson's aircraft was completing a manoeuvre at Chicksands it failed to pull out of its dive and crashed, killing the pilot. It goes without saying that everyone in the Wing was devastated. Not too long after the crash instructions were given to make a sign worded "Thompson Drive" to be installed at the crossroads adjacent to Building 136, in honour of the late Colonel. Thereafter the road from the Base entrance gate past Hangar 45 to the Ivy Lodge road junction would be known by the name of this popular aviator.

At this point I should mention Ipswich Town Football Club and its many American Air Force supporters who passed through the turnstiles every weekend, having been introduced to English Football by their English girlfriends. Among the Ipswich players in those days were Mick Mills, George Burley and Dave Johnson, to name but three. Fhe Bentwaters supporters club was so enthusiastic that the players were invited up to the Officers Club for special occasions, to appreciate the enthusiastic support that the US Airmen and their wives and girlfriends were offering. The couple who were mainly responsible for organising these special gatherings were M/Sergeant Steve Schafer and his Ipswich-born wife Jackie. They were occasions, I'm sure, that Mick Mills and his teammates would have enjoyed and appreciated.

Colonel Rudolph Wacker had been the Wing Commander for the past 27 months and was moving on. Colonel Gordon E. Williams would be the new Wing Commander until mid-1981. All these Wing Commanders occupied the large bungalow within the on-base housing complex. Some of the 'first ladies' found things very much to their liking and others requested minor changes.

I have to say that I remember Mrs Williams taking over the residence and making all manner of requests for changes. As I was on the spot with the BCE Squadron it was for me to leave my programming post for a short while and don my other hat to make Mrs Williams see the difficulty in complying with some of her requests, hoping that she wouldn't keep up the pressure and exercise her authority to make life too difficult. Fortunately, we overcame most problems.

After completing my three years on secondment with the BCE Squadron it was time for me to get back to the quality control job that suited me best. I programmed many projects into the system that were funded in the 1980s. The Hardened Shelter project was not moving too well so I would not join the Part 1 Shelter team. The Government had now changed the name of our Department from Ministry Public Building Works (MPBW) to Property Services Agency (PSA). I would pick up the role of Maintenance control officer at Wethersfield, where the USAF Red Horse Team was based. This was a team of American airmen with all the equipment to carry out Rapid Runway Repair (RRR), a very well trained group of military personnel who would demonstrate the rapid repair and were also into carrying out building maintenance work of all trades.

There was serious trouble with the Shelter Project due to a dispute between the Main Contractor and his Sub contractor which went on for many months, delaying the completion of the Shelters and handover to the USAF; leaving everything in building site conditions far longer than was forecast. Eventually the Ministry Project Manager was obliged to hire a new independent contractor at no additional cost to the client to complete the unfinished shelters. A statement later by 'the man from the ministry' declared that this industrial dispute had been the worst encountered in the history of government contracts.

The runways on the Twin Bases were due for a major overslab once again and would be closed to flying as they alternated to get the necessary work scheduled. Some of the aircraft rotated to the forward bases in Germany, which incorporate exercises with other military services. This overslab at Bentwaters would add eight inches of additional surface material to the main runway, taking it to 32 inches in total thickness. With aircraft like F4Ds landing their 20 ton weight with a tyre pressure of 250 PSI this runway thickness was necessary.

Remember the sports field that Colonel Wacker so cleverly hired from the local farmer? Well, there was an idea that this field would make a very good site for some urgently needed Married Family Houses. An application was made and everyone expected approval to be given for approximately 90 (MFH) units, in the main 2/3 bedroom houses for the use of Service Families at Bentwaters. It would take away the sport facilities that all age groups had enjoyed but the need for MFH

was so great that sacrifices would have to be made. A scheme for the new houses would be drawn up to lease the 90 units over a 10-year period. It would be some time before the project got the go ahead.

Meanwhile the construction of housing units for the Bentwaters Air Force Families at Saxmundham and Grundisburgh had been given the go ahead. This would be on a 10-year hire agreement and would help ease the housing shortage problem again.

As we reach 1981 Colonel Richard M. Pascoe takes the Wing for the next 18 months. The past Wing Commanders have worked their socks off submitting projects to obtain approval and funding for submittal to the PSA. The PSA would be working hard to finalise drawings and tender documents. Approval would be given to a large number of new facilities and the 1980s would be a very busy decade.

To begin with we were to start the construction of a complete new hospital on an area that until now had been part of an agricultural field. The deal that had been done was to hand the old wartime Site 6 back to the local farmer and in return take part of a field adjacent to the new Airmen's barracks on Site 7. The wartime huts had been deliberately dispersed with a field separating each site to reduce their vulnerability to aerial attack. The field between sites would now become the new Hospital site. This would release the old hospital site to become available for the new Mission Support Building to be constructed towards the late 1980s.

Other projects getting the go ahead were the Airfield Arm and De-arm Revetments for aircraft at both ends of the active runway. These were large, metal, soiled-filled, box-type constructions at least as high as the A10 itself, to give adequate protection against any mishap.

There was a need for a landing and take-off strip running parallel with the main-runway 150 yards to the south. This would provide an alternative for aircraft to use should a problem arise with the main 08-26 runway. This new concrete parallel emergency strip would be part of a contract when the South West Aircraft Parking Development was approved for funding in 1982.

The South West Development was a 250-acre area of extra Forestry Commission land. It had taken the USAF top brass a lot of negotiating and planning to get this additional area of forestry land for additional aircraft parking dispersals. The Forestry Commission workforce would fell and clear away the trees.

Another ongoing project was the new Permanent Victor Alert Crew building, a facility for which we had been requesting funds for some time. Up to this time only temporary office and living accommodation has been available. The building was a 24-hour facility operating with aircrew on alert standby duties, which was all part of the NATO operating requirements. There were other small ongoing ancillary projects at, for example, the Tanker Shop Office, the Ground Power Shop extension and the extension to the Motor Pool Complex. The Part 1 Works Resident Engineer and his staff of technical officers were very involved supervising these million dollar projects.

The A10s had returned to flying at Bentwaters following the completion of the runway resurfacing and were busy operating and training in their capacity as tank-busters. There were aircraft in the sky almost continuously. 509 and 511 Squadrons were programmed to move to Alconbury in the late 1980s, leaving the 510 Squadron as a 4th Squadron within the 81st Wing.

Colonel Dale C. Tabor took over as Wing Commander from August 1982 to March 1984. This would be a busy time for the new Wing Commander as there would be several new projects receiving funding approval to add to the existing new structures already in progress.

The 2nd Top Four Club / Open Mess would get the go ahead, as would the new Sports Centre, both projects at Bentwaters, while the High School at Woodbridge would get their long awaited Gym. The new aircraft hard standing dispersals project in the South West Development had now been given a start date.

A new Flight Simulator was planned to be sited on the south side of the Flight line adjacent to the Maintenance Control Facility. It may appear to the reader that a tremendous amount of building is going on and it is.

Even though we were now in the 1980s, the situation with regard to the Cold War remained largely unchanged since 81st Fighter Tactical Wing had arrived in the 1950s. Projects that previous Colonels and their squadron personnel had planned and submitted to the Base Civil Engineer's Department in the 1960s and 70s for funding were now getting approval. NATO was keeping up the pressure to maintain an efficient air force to be deployed as and when required, and the 81st Wing would continue to be ready to meet the challenge.

It was also in the 1980s that the Wing Commanders of the 81st declared their dislike for the drab colour scheme of the buildings on the Twin Bases. They suggested that most buildings would be more acceptable with a cream exterior with flashes of chocolate across the centre or on the doors to break up the outline and we all agreed that they looked better after this had been done.

When HQ USAFE selected the 81st Wing to operate the A10 Tankbuster, four bases were then chosen to serve as forward operating locations. Det 1 at Sembach AB, Det 2 at Leipheim, Det 3 at Ahlhorn and Det 4 at Norvenich. Three were German bases and Sembach was already a main operating base for USAF F-111 aircraft. With the change weapons system also came two more squadrons – the 509th and the 511th – making six operational fighter squadrons operating

In addition to her award certificate, Colonel Cranskog presented Iris with an 81st Wing plaque [USAF]

DEPARTMENT OF THE AIR FORCE

PRESENTS THE AWARD

FOR MERITORIOUS CIVILIAN SERVICE

TO

IRIS M. FLETCHER

CITATION:

Mrs Iris M. Fletcher is awarded the Meritorious Civilian Service Medal for her outstanding service while employed by the British Ministry of Defense, for the United States Air Force, 81st Civil Engineering Squadron, 81st Combat Support Group, Royal Air Force Bentwaters, England, during the period July 1982 through July 1983. Her exceptional managerial and financial skills resulted in major contributions to the effectiveness and success of the base mission. The distinctive accomplishments of Mrs Fletcher reflect great credit upon herself, the British Ministry of Defense, and the United States Air Forces in Europe.

Billy M.Minter

BILLY M. MINTER
General, USAF
Commander in Chief
United States Air Forces in Europe

from the East Suffolk Twin Base complex. Because of its large size, the 81st racked up thousands of flying hours and sorties. In the fiscal year 1982 the Wing flew 53,391 hours, to set a peacetime tactical air force record for hours flown by a Wing. In 1986 another record was set when Wing aircrews and maintenance personnel launched 105 of 118 assigned aircraft.

As was stated earlier, to obtain funding one required good sound projects and the best finance section you could employ in the (BCE). The 81st had been very fortunate in having Mrs Iris Fletcher as head of that section. The USAF recognised this good fortune and was ready to award Iris with the highest award that the Air Force could bestow on a civilian. Iris received her Award

Certificate and Medal from Colonel Tabor the Wing Commander at a specially arranged retirement function in the Officers Club. Iris was also presented with many squadron goodies with their thanks. We all had a nice evening and it was an honour to be there.

With the amount of money being spent at Bentwaters and the increasing number of new buildings being completed, Suffolk County Council was planning to extend the Base bypass road towards Eyke, cutting off the dangerous School Meadow Bend, also known as "dead man's corner" that led to the old Rendlesham School and Norton Hall. Over the years many vehicles had slid off that sharp bend into the adjacent deep drainage ditch. This new road extension would afford right and left hand turning lanes for Friday Street, the Officers Club and the Tower field.

Costing in the order of £700,000 it would be a vast improvement to the A1156 and benefit the flow of through traffic to Snape and Tunstall. This very worthwhile project was due for completion in the second half of the 1980s. The road through the village of Eyke was well used and now upgraded to an 'A-class' road, fitted out with street lighting and resurfaced. It would have been of benefit of everyone if a link road between RAF

Bentwaters and RAF Woodbridge had somehow been agreed and put into effect but this was never taken too seriously.

At Woodbridge Base during the early 1980s the Deputy Base Commander, Lieutenant Colonel Charles Halt was involved in an alleged UFO sighting.[1] The UFO was supposed to have landed in Rendlesham Forest adjacent to Woodbridge base. A number of airmen were also involved, which made the incident more credible. I have no thoughts about this myself and leave the subject to those who were involved. Some of those who were based here at that time remember the incident, as the following letters confirm.

My two oldest daughters were arrested by a Colonel Charles Halt of the UFO Rendlesham Incident. They too departed the base near the Officers Housing Area on Bentwaters. Pam and I had to go to the Police desk and gain their release. Where was Ray Young when I needed him? He was five years too late.

Cheers Ron And Pam Burrell

My father was stationed at Bentwaters from 1978-84. I went too and graduated from Woodbridge School. During that time we lived in Marlesford, Framlingham and on Woodbridge base. We were living on the base during the famous (or infamous) UFO incidents in 1980. I remember Col. C. Halt, the Deputy Base Commander, very well. In fact, my mother was his secretary.

---

[1] In late December 1980 there was a series of reported sightings of unexplained lights near Rendlesham Forest, Suffolk, England. The events occurred just outside RAF Woodbridge, used at the time by the US Air Force. USAF personnel including deputy base commander Lieutenant Colonel Charles I. Halt claimed to see things they described as a UFO sighting. The occurrence ranks among the best-known reported UFO events worldwide. The Ministry of Defence (MoD) stated, however, that the event posed no threat to national security and it was never investigated as a security matter. The sightings were explained as a misinterpretation of a variety of nocturnal lights, a fireball, the Orford Ness lighthouse or bright stars. (*source* Wikipedia, 2016)

I would like very much to return to Britain and see how much has changed since I was last there.

Cheers Chuck Ross

It is interesting that over 20 years on, nothing more has been heard or seen of the UFO and very few wish to comment on the subject. I was asked to comment by the BBC TV assistant director of the programme *UFO Mystery* shown in 2003 but declined.

The Wing Commander from March 1984 to March 1986 would be Colonel Lester P. Brown Jr. Colonel Brown would have the pleasure of taking over a number of new completed buildings and witness the start of the airfield extension as the South West Development for additional aircraft parking got underway. The new emergency runway strip also got the go ahead with its connections to the existing taxiway.

The new L-shaped Base Civil Engineers and (PSA) Property Services Agency combined offices was almost complete. The (BCE) left Building 555 to the Drafting/Drawing section and Mrs Iris Fletcher and her accountant officers.

Another project was to replace the Wing Commander's office accommodation. He was still operating out of the wartime tin huts on Site 1 at RAF Bentwaters. Previous wing commanders had offered many ideas and suggestions but had moved on without there being much action in this regard. Now there was hope for a move and a project was put up for funding to move the Wing Commander's office to the Flight Line on Thompson Drive.

The Communication Squadron office was planned to be modified and become one of the smartest buildings on the base. The Comm Squadron did not like moving but the scheme was approved by HQ USAFE and funding would follow. The roof of the new Comm. Building would be redesigned by (PSA) Property Services Agency from a flat roof to a pitched roof for the redesigned upstairs layout. PSA would also design a hardened structure so that the Wing Commander's urgent alert duties could continue to function even during troubled times.

Throughout the 1980s and into the 1990s the Base would take on a new look as new structures rose above the skyline and everyone was to benefit from the added facilities.

The BCE Programmes Section submitted a project for a new Mission Support Squadron Building on the site of the old wartime hospital. The old site huts were to be cleared and a new car park area prepared to serve the new building. I had been transferred to PSA Woodbridge Sub-district Office for the next three years; I would be replacing the outgoing officer who had reached the retirement age set by the Civil Service.

It is worth mentioning that the massive building programme such as sports and leisure facilities ongoing at Bentwaters was intended to serve the majority of 81st Wing personnel, including those on Woodbridge base.

RAF Woodbridge Rifle Range, used by the entire Wing personnel, obtained funding for refurbishment and additional safety features for public protection. This heavily used range (not to be mistaken for the wartime Bromeswell Range) was the only facility on the north side of the Woodbridge runway, being isolated in a wooded area and on the edge of the airfield boundary, adjacent to a public footpath, so safety was a top priority.

Also at Woodbridge, the new High School Gym was almost complete, constructed by AMEC Contractors. This would be welcomed by both the School Principal and the Military, who would now have the Woodbridge Base Gym to themselves. They had been sharing this lone gym and it was not a happy arrangement.

The 81st Comptroller Squadron was activated in 1st August 1985. This Squadron would provide financial services to host and tenant units; collect, distribute and account for appropriated funds; advise commanders and train resource managers; prepare and execute budgets; conduct economic and cost analyses; and administer the internal review program, management information systems and respond to audits.

The PSA at Bentwaters had a new District Works Officer (DWO). The DWO was the opposite number to the BCE and they worked very well together. Mr Woods took up the post as DWO in 1984 from Mr Fred Nalton, who had succeeded the late Mr Roy Piper. We had a retirement lunch in 1980 for Mr Piper, attended by the Base Commander, Area Officer (Mr Corbit) and others, at the Melton Grange Hotel; everyone was grateful for his 13 years' service at Bentwaters. Mr Nalton moved on in 1984 to Greenham Common (to deal with the lady protesters, presumably; any damage caused by these people had to be corrected by the PSA). The last report I saw about Mr Nalton pictured him standing outside Buckingham Palace with a well-earned medal that he had just received from Her Majesty.

Another new squadron was the 81st Mission Support Squadron, activated on 7th September 1986, to provide support to commanders, 5,000 Air Force members and their dependents, and 350 civilian employees at two main operating bases in England and four forward operating locations in Germany, responsible for administrative and human resource programs.

The number of the main runway at Bentwaters had changed from 08-26 to 07-25. This was due to the fact that over a period of around 40 years magnetic north varies slightly so the old numbering was no longer correct for flying purposes.

At Woodbridge the High School was filling up with new students who had been receiving their education either in Germany or other USAF schools in the U.K. With the classroom extensions completed and sports facilities now more readily available it was considered appropriate that every student should enjoy US-style schooling, albeit with some British teachers.

There was an accident involving an A10 aircraft of the 510th Squadron from Woodbridge Base. The A10 was on exercise over The Wash when it developed engine trouble. the pilot, Lieutenant Colonel William Olsen baled out and was awaiting rescue in very rough water. An RAF Wessex rescue helicopter arrived on the scene and the RAF Warrant Officer winchman was lowered down to rescue the Colonel. It is understood that the parachute and harness around the Colonel was proving difficult to free from his flying suit. The rough seas were not helping our Warrant Officer and the weight for the Wessex was proving too much. Such was the strain on the cable that it snapped and left the Wessex without any contact with the two men. With the North Sea never being too warm at any time it was important that some other means of rescue was found quickly.

The Woodbridge 67th Squadron Jolly Green Giant Rescue Helicopter went to the scene and picked up the two airmen but sadly they were pronounced dead on arrival on dry land.

Nanette and Alexandra Olsen.

This was a very sad occasion for the whole Wing. It will be remembered that back in the 1970s the pilot William Olsen had met and married our very own Miss Anglia Nanette Slack after a whirlwind romance. They had enjoyed travelling around the world, serving at the various US Air Force bases as a very happy couple. I happened to be in the vicinity of the Woodbridge Chapel on the morning of the funeral for the Colonel and remember seeing Nanette with her daughter Alexandra (see picture above) and son Tony by her side on this very sad occasion. As far as I know Nanette now lives in Ipswich. Alexandra became a professional dancer in the US and is happily married to a handsome American.

The RAF Wessex helicopter was unable to cope with the rough seas. [IWM]

Peak Performance – 1986-91

It was now 35 years since the 81st Wing had arrived at Bentwaters and everything had come a long way since that September day in 1951. The Wing Commander from March 1986 to July 1987 would be Colonel William A. Studer. There were now 10,000 people involved with the Twin Bases, mostly American servicemen and women and their families. In addition over 350 civilian workers were making a contribution to running the Bases in non-military service jobs, all helping to keep the wheels turning.

In common with other recent commanders, Colonel Studer would be welcoming a number of new projects which had been implemented due to the large number of people now living and working on the Twin Bases. For example, a drive-in Burger King and a Beer Store at Bentwaters, home from home comforts for the troops. It was now clear that despite all the MFH we already had on both bases and including Wacker Field in planning to come, it would be necessary to plan for even more Married Quarters to meet the demand. The Commander should have his personnel living close to the base and be part of emergency military backup. The Tower Field, as we called it, was adjacent to the Wing Commanders Quarters and the subject of an MFH project to increase the number of units available to wing personnel. Further to this, an application was made to build 200 new government-funded MFH units at the west end of Woodbridge airfield adjacent to the Hollesley public road as a matter of urgency.

A second Arrestor Barrier was to be installed further up the runway from the existing barriers; this is presumably to take over should the first barriers at each end fail.

Let's just give the wing personnel who serve at the Forward Bases a mention.

Maintenance ground crew had just about finished pre-flight checks on the last of the squadron's A10s, topping off the LOX and signing off the exceptional releases. The weatherman had briefed the pilots to expect gradually clearing skies, the result of a cold front moving in from the North Atlantic. As the morning sky brightened, the first pilots stepped into their jets. One would think this a typical winter morning for the world's largest tactical fighter wing? It was not exactly.

Actually, a small part of the Wing was starting its day at the 81st Tactical Fighter Wing's Detachment 4, Norvenich, West Germany. Because each of the Wing's four German forward operating locations must be prepared to operate independently during a conflict, all support functions must be in place and operational. Each FOL must be prepared to function as a small wing. The total manning at any detachment was never more than 80 people and being all skilled men it made life difficult should one or more report sick. As the Colonel in charge says, "It's certainly not always easy for our people being so isolated from military facilities." Nevertheless Norvenich was one of the best of the four FOL bases from which to plan trips to the rest of Europe.

The relationship between Det 4 and its German host, the 31st Fighter Bomber Wing, was close. It had to be, because NATO Tactical Evaluation inspected both units as a team. In fact, Det. 4 would become the 3rd Squadron of this German Wing in the event of hostilities.

This unique relationship resulted in many Det. 4 people working side by side with their German counterparts. "We are all skilled people here." The Colonel continues. "We've got just about every responsibility that Bentwaters has, with the exception of security police, and that's provided by the Germans."

It wasn't just Americans and Germans at the FOLs. One English guy I should tell you about is Ted Warner. Ted was a sheet metal worker of great skill who began working at Bentwaters in the early 1960s. Since the Air Ministry Works Department (AMWD) did not use sheet metal as a material he moved to the USAF civilian staff organisation, where he linked up with the military and, after much security screening, worked on the Phantoms and A10s. Ted, who lived in Woodbridge town, proved to be a wizard in the art of working sheet metal, so much so that the Equipment Maintenance Squadron (EMS) bosses asked him to serve at the Forward Bases in Germany

from time to time. Ted would enjoy the experience of travel and working in different environments. He worked on all four FOLs throughout the period of 1970s and 1980s and had many a story to tell on his return to the UK and his normal place of work was in the Aircraft Hangars at the twin Bases.

The summer of 1987 brought a new Wing Commander, Colonel Harold H. Rhoden, the 29th Wing Commander of the 81st since WW2. The 81st Wing was now the largest Wing serving in Europe and one of the most efficient, according to the awards collected in recent years.

The 67th ARRS at Woodbridge were equally well placed as an efficient military force; they had just been joined by the 21st Special Operations Squadron to support US military special operation forces by providing resupply and airlift. The 67th would phase out their HH-53 helicopters, which would be passed to the 21st Squadron, who would continue to provide humanitarian assistance and may be tasked for combat rescue support. In essence the 67th would be

Ted Warner (8th from right) joins members of 510th Squadron and a couple of A-10 aircraft for a photo call.

responsible for the operation of the C-130s and the 21st would operate the HH-53s.

The following text from the base newspaper called *Forum* gives some indication of the type of exercises that the 81st Tactical Fighter Wing got involved in during their training.

Bentwaters joins in with mock attacks.

A five-day exercise named "Osex 15" involving low flying aircraft was staged by the RAF in Wales, Monday through Thursday. During the exercise RAF Jaguars, Tornados and Harriers together with 43 A-10s from Bentwaters made mock attacks on targets within an exercise area North of Lampeter and Llandovery and south of Newton and Machynlleth. The purpose of the exercise was to train RAF aircrews and RAF/Army forward air controllers in providing offensive support for forces on the ground. Tornado F3, Phantom, Hawk and Lightning fighter aircraft and Rapier and Javelin ground to air missile units played the 'enemy' defending the exercise area. Up to 110 sorties were flown each day. Aircraft were restricted to flying no lower than 250ft and mainly no faster than 450 knots. Some exercise traffic also flew on to ranges at Castle Martin, Sennybridge and Pembroy.

As was stated earlier the 509th and the 511th Squadrons would move to Alconbury and each Squadron got a new Squadron commander to take them to their new base. 509 Squadron, known as 'the Pirates' were led by Lieutenant Colonel Jerry Raper and 511th Squadron, known as 'the Vultures' would be led by Lieutenant Colonel Jack Shafer.

There were other changes during Wing Commander Colonel Hal Rohden's term of office. The Wing Commander himself settled into his new office adjacent to the flight line; the twin flagpoles flying the Stars & Stripes and the RAF Standard were relocated beside Thompson Drive for the everyday raising and lowering ceremony; the new Hospital Clinic provided a very important service for Wing personnel and their dependants; and the New Sports Centre was up and running for all sports enthusiasts.

Taking this base newspaper "Forum" a stage further and how the USAF Safety personnel on base try to offer advice to their people on road safety. This is a brief extract from the Safety column.

Hazards have always been pointed out to US drivers. The village of Eyke and 'Dead Man's Corner' are two of the better known ones in the area. In the village of Snape there's a shop used by local children which is hidden from view to approaching traffic. Anxiety has been expressed regarding the excessive speed of some vehicles in this area. Make sure it is not you that is apprehended for speeding. A new 'priority' sign on the bridge at Sternfield gives priority to oncoming traffic but this is not always observed; if you are not sure of its meaning consult the Highway Code. Blaxhall residents are concerned that Saxmundham traffic is using the village as a shortcut which they would prefer did not happen, so please co-operate in making their village safer.

I found myself on the centre pages of the May 1987 edition of *Forum* because, after 44 years working on airfields, I was about to retire. I felt OK but at 60 years of age I was officially too old to continue working for the Government. Well, we all have to go sometime; now it was my turn. All was not lost, however, because I could carry on working, if I wanted to, as an employee of one of the firms of consultants that worked on the airfields. I may be back, we would see... Meanwhile I would keep in touch with the activities on the Twin Bases and carry on writing. Sergeant Dawn McKee said some nice things about me, referring mainly about my stories of the past which you have been reading. Lieutenant Colonel Jack Baker, the Base Civil Engineer at the time of my retiring, presented me with a "Can Do" award, which was a very nice thought by him and his team.

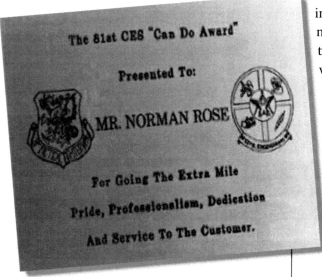

The 81st CES "Can Do Award"

Presented To:

MR. NORMAN ROSE

For Going The Extra Mile

Pride, Professionalism, Dedication
And Service To The Customer.

It would be treasured for all time. So many awards were handed out by the squadron commanders in appreciation for what I, and many others on the receiving end of awards, had done while on the job.

Colonel Tad J. Oelstrom was the new Wing Commander from summer 1988. Tad had been heavily involved in a variety of sports at the Twin Bases. During his time as WC he would take over many more new facilities as they were completed and arrange for them to be handed over for use. The Wacker Field Housing project was ongoing, with 1990 as the occupation takeover timeframe. This and the Tower Field Development for the American service families would be managed by a consortium with a 10 year lease agreement.

I was back at work after a short break, working for AMEC, the construction contractor, but covering the same projects I would have covered if still working for PSA. One of these projects was the refurbishment of the Woodbridge Airmen's Barracks. Some time ago I mentioned that the airmen were unhappy about the barrack blocks having a central corridor and how a project must be applied for and funded to change the floor layout. The entrance to each room would be from the exterior. A steel frame would be mounted on the outside to support a walkway and the inside corridor would be converted into a shower and toilet cubical for each room. These changes promised to be a vast improvement on the original layout. No more late night shouting and singing in that dreaded central corridor. Everyone welcomed this project.

Summer Hire was a programme of employing school students aged 16 years or over during the school summer vacation. Most of the work undertaken by students involved cleaning, painting and repairs, although some clerical jobs would be available. The applicants must be members of a US military family and would earn $2.90 per hour. The summer break was for at least two months to give the teachers an opportunity to visit the States. The school bus contractor got to enjoy a break also. Belle Coaches always managed to organise every summer trip for the local people come what may.

We had seen the 509th and 511th Squadrons deploy to Alconbury and arrangements were made to welcome the 527th Aggressor Squadron, flying their F16 Fighting Falcons in practice combat with the A10s. The painting of the Russian Bear on the Aircraft Shelter door was something different and just illustrated the sense of humour of our American neighbours.

It was the turn of the Security Police Squadron to get a new facility complete with new control room and detention cells that would meet the standards expected in the 1980s and 1990s. The new Police Control building would be located on the site of the old cottage that Lottie and I had once lived in, just inside the main entrance gate to the airfield. It was nice that the construction of this new building would not affect the two holly trees standing in what had been our front garden. The new structure was programmed for completion in the early 1990s.

The Government had given approval for an additional 200 Married Family Housing units to be constructed on the west end of Woodbridge Airfield. These would be funded and managed by the Property Services

Agency (PSA), unlike the Bentwaters Wacker Field and Tower Field MFH projects, which were Housing Consortiums. It's great news for the Air force personnel who will take over the quarters in 1990.

Meanwhile the F16 Fighting Falcons Aggressor Squadron were going about the business of playing the part of the enemy and taking the practice fight to the A10 Squadrons.

Here is an interesting piece from the base newspaper *Forum* in 1988.

"Turning bullets to bucks"

Sale of spent casings brings money back to 81st (MWR) Morale, Welfare, Recreation.

As submitted by Captain George Morris.

Each time an 81st Tactical Fighter Wing pilot presses the trigger, he sends a stream of 30mm bullets toward a target. He also produces mounds of spent shell casings. It doesn't take long for mounds to turn into mountains. Last year, for example, the 81st TFW expended 832,035 rounds of 30mm target practice ammunition; each round produced an empty shell which had to be disposed of. Enter the conventional munitions maintenance shops of the 81st Equipment Maintenance Squadron. "In the past, we took the spent shells to RAF Molesworth," said TSgt. Chris Lacey, non-commissioned officer in charge of the Bentwaters conventional section. "We eventually saturated its scrap yard and it wasn't long before Molesworth couldn't accommodate us." Sergeant Lacey, along with TSgt. Ross Backe, assistant NCOIC of the RAF Woodbridge conventional munitions shop, made countless phone calls and coordinated with the Defence Reutilization and Marketing Office at Molesworth. Their effort eventually resulted in the direct sale of the spent casings to private contractors. The first mountain of casings totalled 101.2 tons of scrap metal worth $39,806. It was hauled away June 1987. But pilots kept pulling triggers and spent casings continued to pile up in the munitions branch. More recently a second contract was coordinated. It was carried off by a stateside contractor to the tune of $43,870.

"It takes a lot of work to put one of these contracts together," said Sgt. Lacey. "It's worth the effort because our wing benefits from the sale of the scrap."

Sergeant Lacey's comments were almost an understatement. A total of $82,596 has been realized through the initiatives of people like him and Sgt. Backe. The money is fed back to the 81st TFW for Morale, Welfare and recreation support. Some money is going toward new equipment for the Bentwaters bowling centre and snack bar.

"EMS delivers," said Sergeant Backe, "whether its bombs, bullets or bucks."

My Wife Lottie retired in March 1990 after 17 years as a clerical officer in the PSA Office. The American Captain and Mr Ainsley the PSA District Works Officer said 'thank you' at

the office presentation (see photo below).

In Summer 1990 and Colonel Oelsrtrom handed the Wing over to Colonel Roger E. Carlton. It would be a very busy time for Roger Carlton as he took control of many more completed facilities handed over through PSA to the squadrons. It may be surprising that there was still a continuous stream of new buildings available at this stage, 40 years after the USAF had arrived at the Bentwaters base but the machinery of approval and funding of the various projects had turned very slowly in some cases.

Every airman who had passed through the Twin Bases had worked towards improve the facilities and nothing was going to stop them now. We had seen new Aircraft Shelters, a new Headquarters Development and a New Hospital to name but a few. Also slated for construction was a New Security Police HQ, a new Mission Support Facility close to the Bentwaters by-pass roundabout, a New Community Centre adjacent to the Theatre and a new Post Office to be located on the site of the old, clapped-out Gym.

At Woodbridge in addition to the 200 MFH units under construction, three new Barrack Blocks were to be built and the school buildings were to be upgraded. Mr Seligman

was Principal at Woodbridge High School at that time.

The Bentwaters Wacker Field MFH construction was ongoing and the Tower Field MFH project had been approved, great news for the commanders, who would now have all their key personnel near at hand if any emergency arose.

The refurbished Barrack Blocks at Woodbridge were handed back to the Squadron personnel, who were delighted with the changes that had been made. I was now attending to the supervision of the remainder of the 200 Woodbridge MFH, the previous supervisor having moved on to another project. I read in the specification for the housing that waterbeds were not permitted. I'm not sure how many airmen were planning on installing one but just as well to be safe. Waterbeds can be excessively heavy weight is not recommended in these units.

The Bentwaters runway was due for resurfacing. It was 10 years since any surface treatment had been applied to the 9000 foot long monster and in 1990/91 it would be closed to all flying. It was expected that the resurfacing would be completed in 1990, dependent on the British summer weather.

527th F16 Aggressor Squadron would soon be departing. [USAF]

The refurbished barrack block at Woodbridge was a great improvement. [USAF]

We had fewer aircraft at this time with the 527th F16 Aggressor Squadron departing and 509 and 511 squadrons now operating out of Alconbury. And the Forward Bases would now play an important part in the A10 flying programme. Construction work at Bentwaters was at an all-time high, with a number of contractors being awarded various projects. The PSA Resident Engineer Richard Sherrill was a busy man in his office at the Butley Gate end of the Base, keeping abreast with all the different queries and arranging monthly progress meetings to suit each contractor.

AMEC were resurfacing the concrete ends of the runway, with an asphalt specialist sub-contractor handling the resurfacing of the main centre stretch of 'blacktop'.

The summer turned out to be a good one and everyone was hopeful that flying would resume at Bentwaters in autumn 1990. We noticed that there was a lot more flying from Woodbridge during the Bentwaters runway closure. It was truly an advantage to have the use of the twin airfields, rotating the squadrons to maintain the Wing's flying commitments. I linked up with other members

of staff to supervise the remainder of the resurfacing work before I called it a day. While out there surveying the newly-laid surface I noticed an A10 taking off from the new emergency strip completed only a couple of years previously and was surprised but delighted for the Wing that this new strip could be used on these occasions. The Woodbridge runway may be slated for re-surfacing later.

Anyway, it was time for me to leave in order to relax and put my feet up. I had enjoyed the additional two and half years doing what I liked doing best, but now I would have time to get on the computer and start writing (this book).

Colonel Carleton was ready to take the airfield back on behalf of the Wing and to welcome the squadrons back to their base with a reinstated flying programme. As we entered 1991 the new Community Centre adjacent to the theatre was rising fast up into the skyline and the large Mission Support Facility adjacent to the roundabout was making progress. You will remember that when the first 300 MFH units began construction, I referred to a smelly old wartime sewage pump house that would remain in the midst of them (and be within one of the property gardens). Now a long-awaited rectification of this malodorous state of affairs was taking place. A new sewage ejector pump was installed to serve the new Support Building and would include diverting the old wartime drainage system and demolishing that awful beast at long last. What a relief that must have been to the nearby residents!

The year 1991 saw a dangerous situation arise in the Middle East when the Iraqis led by Sadaam Hussein invaded neighbouring Kuwait. In response US President George Bush Snr announced that a task force would be deployed to liberate Kuwait and remove the Iraqi forces. Operation "Desert Storm" was about to commence and would involve Squadrons of A10s from the 81st Wing. All wing personnel were ready for the challenge. Under Commander-in-Chief General Norman Schwarzkopf, US forces would be joined by armed forces of many other nations and it was expected that the war, which would come to be known as The Gulf War, would be over quite quickly.

The conflict was not without controversy and an incident involving 'friendly fire' from USAF A10s onto our British tanks made the headlines, triggering Stormin' Norman's famous response, "You know what? Our boys have got to live with that for the rest of their lives."

81st Wing A10s were still operating a watchful eye in that area for several months after the ceasefire. There was a very nice homecoming picture in the Base newspaper *Forum* of Captain Bruce McClintock, a 91st Squadron pilot, being greeted by his wife Tamara and family as the squadron returned from Dhahran in Saudi Arabia in late 1991 (shown right).

The 510th Squadron deployed to Saudi Arabia replacing the 91st to continue the air observatory support.

There was a mention earlier of the Martlesham Communications site known as the "ROC". Well, in May 1991 the 250 communications people there became the 81st Communications Squadron, providing all communications, computer, visual information and air traffic control services supporting the 81st Tactical Fighter Wing at two main bases, an operating location at Martlesham Heath, and four forward operating locations in Germany.

July 1991 saw another change of Wing Commander as Colonel Roger Carleton handed the wing over to Colonel Roger R. Radcliff. The new Wing Commander would again be heavily involved with new facilities as they were completed.

Mission Complete – 1991-3

Summer 1991 saw preparations for the September "Air Friendship 91 RAF Bentwaters" and, as everyone was getting down to work on this lovely warm July day, it was announced that all civilians employed at the Twin Bases should attend the Base Theatre at 1pm for a special announcement. What was this all about? Everyone was wondering and 1pm could not come soon for most of the puzzled, happy people. At 1 pm the civilians turned up in their hundreds and the RAF Station Commander, Squadron Leader Peter Rooney took the stage. His announcement was short and to the point.

The Twin Bases would cease to operate as military bases from the middle of 1993. It was expected that the 81st Wing would begin the rundown of the bases in a few weeks' time with a final exit date of 30th August 1993.

After such a shock announcement the closure of the bases was naturally the talking point from here on in. The Iraq War had only just ended – but would it flare up again? With construction of the new MFH on Wacker Field and Tower Field ongoing and the massive building programme on the base, what action was now to be taken? The new 200 MFH at Woodbridge were only just occupied and the three new barrack blocks at Woodbridge were due to be completed soon. It was made clear that all construction work that had been started would be finished and that the new facilities would be taken over and used by Wing personnel. Air Friendship 91 would go ahead and a Hanger Dance would be arranged for the summer of 1992, just like the wartime Glen Miller days.

Here is the flying programme for Friendship 91 – which is noticeably different compared to the 1966 Open House Day.

12.20pm	The Show begins at with the RAF Falcons Parachute Team.
12:35pm	USAF Thunderbirds Ground Ceremony
1:00pm	USAF Thunderbirds Takeoff
1:35pm	USAF Thunderbirds Land
1:55pm	USAF Thunderbirds March-off
1:56pm	USAF F-111 Flyby
1:57pm	USAF F-15 Demonstration
2:08pm	USAF P47 and A-10 Takeoff
2:09pm	Pearl Harbor Memorial Takeoff: B-17, Zero and P40
2:23pm	USAF P-47 and A-10 flyby
2:27pm	P-47 Demonstration
2:32pm	USAF A-10 Demonstration
2:40pm	Battle of Britain Memorial Flight
2:55pm	RAF Tornado GR-1 Demonstration
3:00pm	Security Police Working Dog Demonstration
3:05pm	USAF Corsair and Zero Air Combat Demonstration
3:20pm	P-51 and ME-109 Air Combat Demonstration
3:30pm	USAF Thunderbirds Narrator and USAF C-141 Takeoff
3:35pm	RAF Jetstream Demonstration
3:45pm	RAF Bulldog Demonstration
3:55pm	RAF Jaguar Demonstration
4:05pm	TBM Zero and Hellcat Surprise Attack
4:15pm	RAF Tucano Flyby
4:25pm	Patrouille de France takeoff
5:00pm	Patrouille de France Lands
5:05pm	P-40,Me-109 and P-51 Air Combat Demonstration
5:30pm	USAF Thunderbirds Takeoff
6:00pm	Air Show Ends

The following is a letter from the Wing Commander Colonel R. Radcliff.

As you'll no doubt have noticed today, the flight line of RAF Bentwaters is a beehive of activity with aircraft landing throughout the day and people busily welcoming our visiting aircrews and British guests.

We not only have two of the finest aerial demonstration teams in the world highlighting the show – the USAF Thunderbirds and the Patrouille de France – but also some of NATO's best aircraft and crews. With all the talk of aircraft, however, it is easy to lose sight of why we're having an open house/ airshow.

For more than 50 years our British friends have hosted American airmen on their shores. Our presence, attitude, thankfulness, and yes our airshows, should all be geared toward showing our appreciation and respect for their continued hospitality and graciousness.

More than 60,000 of our neighbours are expected to come through the gates tomorrow, and with them will leave more than 60,000 impressions of the base, the Air Force and Americans in general. I know they will leave confident of our ability to accomplish our mission of preserving the peace and with a deeper sense of unity between the British and American people.

As we look ahead to completing our mission at RAF Bentwaters and RAF Woodbridge, we should take this opportunity to say "thanks" to all the British people who have made Americans feel so welcome for the last five decades. This weekend should be a time for celebration and a renewal of the ties which bind our two nations.

I encourage everyone to take advantage of this opportunity to meet our neighbours, and if you're not working, come out and see the show. I hope to see you at the open house tomorrow!

Col. Radcliff served in the Desert Storm campaign while Vice Wing Commander of the 10th TFW at Alconbury. He was a command pilot with more than 3,500 flying hours in T-37, F-111 and A-10A.

The 81st Wing had collected many efficiency awards during their time at the Twin bases. some are listed below.

81st Tactical Fighter Wing Air Force Outstanding Unit Awards

- March 28, 1959 to June 30, 1961
- July 1, 1961, to Jan. 30, 1963
- June 1, to May 31, 1968
- July 1, 1968 to June, 30 1970
- July 1, 1976 to June 30, 1978
- July 1, 1979 to June 30, 1981
- July 1, 1981 to June 30, 1983
- June 1, 1989 to May 30, 1991
- June 1, 1991 to June 30, 1993

Meanwhile in this autumn period of 1991 many families would be receiving their next assignment. Those that had only recently arrived would take possession of new MFH as they became completed on the Tower Field and or Wacker Field. There was still a year and a half before shutdown and a lot of work to do.

Some of the aircraft were being flown out to Germany for use at USAF bases there. We should not forget that the A-10s of the 81st Wing were still serving in the Middle East Region. Preparations were being made for BSO and PSA staff to take up other posts on other USAF bases in the UK. Also arrangements were in hand for those who wished to take early retirement. Many civilian workers were bitter that Bentwaters and Woodbridge bases have been chosen for closure. Why not Lakenheath? After all, more progress had been made towards upgrading the Twin Bases than many others in the UK. Perhaps the Queen opening the Snape Concert Hall was a factor. From the opening by Her Majesty back in 1967, special notice and arrangements had been required as

The gigantic C-5 Galaxy – seen here at one of the Bentwaters Open Days – could airlift almost anything. [USAF]

regards flying from Bentwaters in order not to disturb the concerts, hardly ideal for military operations or even training exercises in a Cold War situation.

The 420 US civilian employees and the 250 British civilian staff would now have to seek employment elsewhere. For the past few years the 78th and 91st Squadrons had Operated at Woodbridge base and the 92nd and 510th at Bentwaters and all the squadrons had taken in turns at operating from the forward bases on the continent. The closure would commence in April 1992 and all 80 aircraft would have been disposed of by April 1993. The 20 A-10s of the 78th TFS would return to the USA followed by the 91st TFS in July. Woodbridge was due for closure in October 1992. The 510th Squadron was deactivated and the 92nd moved

to the 17th Air Force Germany. The Twin bases would close in August 1993.

We had seen so many different types of aircraft at the Twin Bases and the larger types were very exciting to watch. These included the C119 Twin Boom Box Car, the C-124 Globemaster, the C-133 Cargomaster, the C-130 Hercules, the C141 Starlifter and the C-5 Galaxy.

It had taken several years to find a suitable place at Bentwaters for a loading / offloading ramp for the C-5 Galaxy cargo-lifting aircraft but at last in the late 1980s a spot was chosen was adjacent to the Control Tower at a point where the original wartime runways had intersected. This area was duly strengthened and made suitable for this giant airlifter.

The view from the Bentwaters Control Tower C-5 Galaxy loading/offloading ramp.

One of the regular flights that we would all miss would be the mail plane arriving every morning at 7am. Early workers cycling around the perimeter road at that early hour to open up the snack bar could set their watches by this regular early bird.

Many American families would leave the Suffolk bases with fond memories.

There were those that departed Woodbridge Base who wrote as follows:

There are many fond remembrances of Woodbridge. It has always had a special place in our hearts. We won't forget England. My youngest son Tony (Anthony) was born there. We (actually just me) tease him by calling him a "little bloke". He always gets a smile on his face when we do that. He was too young to remember England Woodbridge but he has always had a desire to travel there. I hope that he would do that. Maybe he would take his mother and father along with his family. God Bless!

Frank Rebnord

I was stationed at RAF Woodbridge from 1970-72 as a Captain (O-3) in the 78th Tactical Fighter Squadron F-4 Phantom II. Our daughter was born at RAF Lakenheath in 1971. We initially lived in Hilly Fields in Woodbridge, then on Colchester Road in Ipswich before being posted to Italy. In addition to our daughter's birth, we have many fond memories of East Anglia and the UK.

Jim D. Adams Hopkinsville, KY

These are just a couple of the nice memories from American families who took the trouble to tell us how much their stay in the UK meant to them during the Cold War.

In the final year of the Twin Bases the last of the newly constructed buildings were completed. The new Community Centre was the type of facility that the USAF personnel and their families could only dream of during their stay on the base. It had a stage with changing rooms for the actors; a reception area and many meeting rooms on two levels. Time was limited to organise large-scale concerts and the like, but the Recreation Services Squadron was determined to put on a show to at least 'christen' the new centre. The Mission Support Building adjacent to the roundabout was occupied by all those who worked for the Base Commander. It was slightly ironic to see the bright new rooms allocated to the Judge Advocate because his old office had lacked proper facilities for most of the 42 years of the Base's history.

The Mission Support Building was completed in the final year of the Twin Bases.

The Hangar Dance held in 1992 was enjoyed by everyone. [EADT]

The closing down of the 81st Wing would mean that the 67th ARRS and the 21st SOS would be deployed from RAF Woodbridge to RAF Alconbury and RAF Mildenhall to continue their special work in USAF Europe.

The Morale, Welfare, Recreation & Services Squadron was formed and activated in September 1992 and provided recreational support for over 10,000 military and dependent people assigned to the 81st Tactical Fighter Wing. The 81st MWRS managed over a dozen facilities on the bases including the officer and enlisted open messes, sports and fitness centres, library and community centre.

The past 42 years of military occupation, with all the planning, designing and constructing that had taken place over that period, had turned the two old wartime airfields into one of the finest Air Force bases in Europe. One could only hazard a guess at how much money had been spent here over the years. Now it was time to leave all these

well-built facilities to whoever had a use for them.

There would be a lot of equipment to disconnect and remove to either another base or back to the USA, although as one Sergeant reminded me, most of the British-made machinery was subject to customs duty and would therefore be returned to the appropriate department.

Colonel Roger Radcliff was the 32nd and last 81st Wing Commander. The 81st Wing would cease to exist as a Fighter Wing after July 1993. May 21st 1993 was the day set for the 'Inactivation Ceremony'. This would be held at Bentwaters. Woodbridge base would close several months earlier.

The Hangar Dance was arranged in Hangar 45 and everyone was invited. The USAF Europe Band provided the music for dancing and we were entertained by a singing group who could have been mistaken for the Andrew Sisters. It is no exaggeration to say

Colonel (later Major General) Roger R. Radcliff was the last 81st Wing Commander. [USAF]

that over 2,000 people attended this dance. Beer flowed freely and food was in good supply. Everyone turned up intent on having a good time and that they certainly did.

After thousands of sorties and flying hours over Turkey, Iraq, Saudi Arabia, and Kuwait, the final elements of the 81st TFW were to return to the United Kingdom on December 8th 1992 to begin draw down finalization actions. The 92nd Tactical Fighter Squadron's last few aircraft touched down on the afternoon of December 8th – marking the last deployment and wartime operation of 81st TFW aircraft prior to the Wing's inactivation in July 1993.

It was fitting for the Wing to end on such a positive note. The Wing's A-10s had ensured safety for hundreds of thousands of people while in the Middle East. The most notable aspect of the American presence cannot be measured by the number of sorties flown or awards won. The most valuable and lasting legacy had been, and would continue to be, the harmonious relationship between the

Twin Bases and their gracious hosts, the good people of Suffolk.

A few months later, on May 21st 1993, the arranged Inactivation Ceremony took place on Bentwaters Flight line with all 9 Support Squadrons in attendance for an unforgettable ceremony.

The Wing Commander addressed all those attending the Ceremony.

Dear friends of the 81st Tactical Fighter Wing

On behalf of Major General Charles D. Link, 3rd Air Force Commander, and the men and women of RAF Bentwaters and RAF Woodbridge.

I welcome you to this historic event. Today we officially commemorate the inactivation of the 81st Tactical Fighter Wing. On July the 1st 1993, the wing would end a 42 year history of excellence in service by the United States at the Twin Bases. However, the friendship that we have shared with our British hosts would continue for many years to come. We have built many close ties with the people of Suffolk, and have shared much through the years. We have been together from the Cold war to the Gulf war, and the completion of the 81st TFW's mission gives testimony to how successful we, as a team have been.

As members of the 81st, we have had the privilege of sharing me a proud heritage. It's a legacy that spans six decades, several campaigns, and numerous countries. Since 1951 when the 81st Fighter-Interceptor Wing began operations at RAF Bentwaters in response to the soviet threat of expansion, we have been an integral part of the NATO alliance, and of East Anglia. Since then, the personnel of the 81st have served with distinction and style in Suffolk. We have valiantly participated in nearly every major world event, when and where needed. Undeniably, our greatest achievement has been our role in the thawing of east and west relations, and the ending of the Cold War.

I'd like to thank the service members, spouses, and civilian employees of today's 81st Tactical Fighter Wing. Without your professionalism and dedication, we could not have completed our mission in the manner that we have. I'm proud of your great performance. I know that you would take with you many fond memories of your service here at RAF Bentwaters and RAF Woodbridge.

On behalf of all those that have served here in Suffolk over the past 42years, I'd like to thank our British neighbours for their hospitality and kindness. It has been an honour and pleasure to have served you and the United States of America in Suffolk, England.

Roger R. Radcliff, Colonel USAF Commander 81st Tactical Fighter Wing.

Between May 21st and August 30th there was much to do. Military equipment and special items would continue to be shipped to the continent or the States, a large amount of office furniture and small items would be made available at a price to the local businesses. AFEES and most of the Recreation facilities were run down and the Commissary would close its doors to the remaining few personnel on Base. Some of the members of the rear-guard had been chosen because they were retiring from the USAF and/or had permanent homes in the UK. On August 30th Sergeant Bob Hale (USAF retired) witnessed the closure of the gates and hand over of the keys to the British Ministry of Defence.

'Mission Complete' and a job well done.[1]

---

[1] The USAF had just three facilities left to rebuild or refurbish to complete the Bentwaters project: a new Post Office, a new Officers Club and refurbishment of Hangar 74. But, as the saying goes, "You can't win 'em all!"

Happy to be back for the reunion following the closure of the Twin Bases [EADT]

What do we do with the bases now?

As far as Bentwaters was concerned, the Government Inspector for the Enquiry, following objections to flying from the airfield as an airport, stated that one of the prime reasons for recommending that no more flying should be allowed from this redundant military air base was to recognise the importance of the Snape Maltings Concert Hall and its connection with the late Benjamin Britten.

It goes without saying that the closure of the twin bases would mean a very large downturn in the local economy. Companies like Belle Coaches, Hudson Signs and Pearce (the metalworkers at Bredfield) to name but three, would find it very difficult to recover from the large reduction in their turnover.

But the story is not quite over yet...

Going back to 1951, when the first F86 Sabre Fighter (of National Guard 116th Squadron) arrived, one of its young pilots, Frank Palmer, remembers the welcome he received in the UK so well. Frank stayed in the USAF (the National Guard were equivalent to our territorials) and rose to the rank of Lieutenant Colonel before retiring. Frank wanted to have a reunion and persuaded his lovely wife Sharon to help him organise the event in 1998 where they live in Sequim, near Seattle, USA.

The reunion went so well they arranged another one the following year. When they wanted to arrange the 2001 reunion it had to be in the UK. The fifty-year reunion celebration for the 50 members who had braved the long journey included coach tours and a visit to London. While on one of the coach tours in mid-week I was looking forward to directing the coach (I was acting as courier) to RAF Shepherds Grove after fish and chips at Dunwich. Over half way to the closed, redundant base (Frank was based there) the coach radio revealed the bad news. It was September 11th and we were halted in our tracks for a while. We carried on with the tour but everyone wanted to get back to the hotel to ring home and be reassured.

Despite everything the 2001 reunion was a great success, rounded off with a tour of Bentwaters, where we witnessed the unveiling of the newly-constructed brick plinth, adjacent to the Control Tower, supporting a special plaque in memory of all those who had served at the base in its 50 years history. Representing the RAF was the late Squadron Leader Cyril 'Sid' Scorer and for the USAF Lieutenant Colonel (Rtd) Frank Palmer. Sid Scorer's daughter Leslie and her husband Doug provided an enjoyable buffet lunch in the building that had once been the HQ of the 81st Tactical Fighter Wing. A banquet attended by many local dignitaries at Woodbridge Abbey School rounded off an enjoyable week, with the Palmers collecting the "Achievement Award "for organising the 2001 reunion.

The 2002 reunion was held at Walton Beach Florida, which I attended and where the Association members made me an honorary member of the 81st TFW. Dayton Ohio was the venue in 2003, which I also attended. Both reunions were most enjoyable and friendly.

Brigadier General (Retd) Ben Cassidy hands me the plaque at Dayton, Ohio. [CW]

I began this book at the village of Iken, where I had been born and baptised 75 years previously and that is where I'd like to finish it. At the 2003 Dayton reunion I was given the responsibility to carry a presentation plaque back to Iken church. General Cassidy (retired) offered me this plaque to convey to the people of Iken his heartfelt thanks for the kindness and warm welcome he had received when he arrived with his staff all those years ago. General Ben Cassidy had rented a cottage near Iken in the early 1950s and remembered how the pilots used the church steeple to line up for landing on the Bentwaters runway.

I arrived back home from the States wondering about the best way to go about the task of presenting this plaque. After much consultation I approached the retired Lieutenant Colonel Park Sims, who remained living close by, to assist me in the presentation of this lovely plaque to the Iken folk. I thought it appropriate that an American should perform this important presentation and I could not have chosen anyone better. The following is a copy of Lieutenant Colonel Sims address.

Remarks for Iken Church Ceremony – 25th November 2003

The 81st Fighter Wing of the United States Air force was home based at the "twin bases" of RAF Bentwaters and RAF Woodbridge for more than 40 years, from its arrival in 1951 until its departure in 1993.

At the peak of its activity in the 1980s, the Wing had more than 100 fighter aircraft and more than 10,000 American servicemen and their families at the two bases. It was the largest fighter wing in the free world. Of these many thousands of Americans, a small percentage lived on base in military housing, but the vast majority lived off-base in the surrounding towns and villages; towns like Ipswich, Woodbridge, Wickham Market and Aldeburgh; villages like Tunstall, Snape and Iken –where we stand today.

These Americans were invariably welcomed by their British hosts and neighbours and many, many Anglo-American friendships (and marriages) resulted, many of which continue to this day. For many of these Americans their time in Suffolk was a high point of their lives, the most enjoyable and most memorable of their military assignments. Some years ago these Americans formed an association of those who had

In appreciation
of your kindness and your gracious
acceptance of our people in your church,
we present this little memento.

This is late in concept but heartfelt
by all of us from our arrival in 1951
and our final departure in 1993.

~ 81st Fighter Wing

served in the 81st Wing, to preserve their fellowship and those memories of their time in England. They called it the 81st Fighter Wing Association; it has a newsletter, a website and a national convention from time to time, to gather and rekindle friendships and memories.

One enduring memory for the earliest members of the 81st Wing in England – those who were here in the 1950s – is the church at Iken, where we gather now. In those early days at RAF Bentwaters, there were apparently fewer aircraft navigation aids than existed later. Indeed, the first arrivals at Bentwaters were helped to find the base and land there by firing of flares, a practice left over from World War II. In those early days the pilots apparently used the church at Iken as a landmark to line themselves up with the Bentwaters runway, the church being a prominent feature in direct line with the runway and a few miles away.

Those Americans who lived in the area also attended the

church for services throughout the years. At the October 2003 convention of the Fighter Wing Association they decided to send a plaque to Iken church, hopefully to be mounted there, as a memento of the role the church played in the early days of Bentwaters flying, and as a thank-you to the people of the surrounding area who so graciously welcomed the visiting Americans into their towns, villages, homes, and lives.

As a former officer of the 81st Wing at Bentwaters, it gives me great pleasure, and a great sense of honour, to present this plaque to Iken church on behalf of the 81st Fighter Wing Association and all the Americans they represent who served at RAF Bentwaters and Woodbridge. I now present this plaque to the Reverend Clifton and Mrs Cooke, the churchwarden. It bears the following simple but eloquent words:

"In appreciation of your kindness and your gracious acceptance of our people in your church we present this little memento. This is late in concept but heartfelt by all of us from our arrival in 1951 until our departure in 1993."

Thank you very much Park.

Park Sims and I hold the plaque in what will be its final location in the church. [EADT]

Two more photos from the plaque presentation at St Botolph's Church, Iken in November 2003.

Left:

The Revd Canon Robert Clifton, accompanied by churchwarden Louise Cooke, accepting the plaque.

Below:

The presentation party (*left to right*): Norman Rose, Bobby Bennett, Bob Hales (Sgt USAF *Ret*), Park Sims (Lt Col USAF *Ret*), Al Brown (Lt Col USAF *Ret*).

The Twin Bases Today (2016 update)

After the MoD had sold Bentwaters to Seabrook Holdings many different ideas were put forward (and refused) for the future use of the huge base. Since the by-pass road split the base into two sections, when it was eventually resold in the main the former airfield became Bentwaters Park and the former domestic site Rendlesham Park.

BENTWATERS AIRFIELD SITE

Local farmers the Kemble family acquired the airfield as an extension to the Wantisden Hall Farm estate. The airfield buildings were leased to businesses and the pavements and runway have been used for filming, motor vehicle rallies and much else.

BENTWATERS DOMESTIC SITE

Most of the military-type buildings, although quite new, were unsuitable for civilian or business use so, with the exception of the Chapel and a few other buildings, demolition was the order of the day to make way for a housing estate. By 2004 almost 100 of the projected 550 new houses were occupied. These were serviced by a new road layout, blending in with the existing houses on Wacker Field, Tower Field, Rendlesham Park and the 64 former married quarters, including the Wing Commander's bungalow.

WOODBRIDGE

The Woodbridge base remained the property of the Ministry of Defence. The Elementary School was taken over by Suffolk County Council Education Department and is now attended by local children. The airfield and technical buildings were fenced off, the High School and some barrack blocks were be demolished to make way for newly constructed dining facilities and living accommodation. In 2004 the Woodbridge base was due for takeover by the Engineering Section of the Parachute Regiment and the Helicopter Army unit at Wattisham.

TWIN BASES ON THE WORLD WIDE WEB

When Linn Barringer, who had moved to Woodbridge in 1994, started a website about the town, he began to receive emails from ex-Bentwaters USAF personnel, asking about the base, which was by then up for sale, so he put a page about RAF Bentwaters on his website. This turned into a saga over the next few years as interest from ex-USAF people continued. Linn took a few photos of the base from outside the fence. Then in 1997, following a request to find a particular house at RAF Woodbridge, the Woodbridge half of the Twin Bases website began. In 1998 Linn joined a group for an on-site tour arranged by Justyn Keeble and guided by Vernon Drane, from which he was able to display 50 new photographs taken from within RAF Bentwaters. Another major contribution of aircraft photographs came from George Pennick, an amateur snapper who had been a frequent visitor to 'commie corner' when the base was active.

Emails and contributions, mostly from former American Twin Bases personnel continued to fuel the growth of the site. Thanks to contributions from website visitors the original 'page or two' became a fascinating display of photographs and memories which make riveting reading. See for yourself at www.Bentwaters.org.[1]

Changes 12 years on in 2016

Since 2004 when I self-published the first edition of *Twin Bases Remembered* many changes to the former base have certainly been evident. The demolition this summer (2016) of the two remaining buildings – the Sports Centre and Recreation/Theatre will complete the base demolition. I expect these sites will become housing in due course. The purpose-built Angel Theatre was first for demolition, although the removal of this first-class facility to make way for a children's play area was, in my view, a mistake. There are now about 800 houses and bungalows covering what are known these days as 'brownfield' sites on the old airfield.

The Base HQ building adjacent the roundabout, completed only shortly before the base closed, is now called Rockford House and is the HQ of Rockford Components (the UK's largest independent provider of wiring, interconnect and system solutions for the defence, aerospace, marine and nuclear industries). Last time I looked it still had the 81st Wing badge on the carpet in the entrance.

The former telephone exchange is amongst the derelict old Wing HQ tin huts.

Since the airfield was taken over by local farmer Bill Kemble numerous small industries have taken up residence in former hangars and dispersals. There are now 20+ companies using the facilities on the old airfield. Bill is keen to be involved with green energy companies, such as Eastern Woodfuels, who manufacture and supply woodchip biofuel, which is delivered to local schools, shops and businesses for woodchip-powered heating. Green energy is also produced from burnable farm waste to generate electricity on site, which is used to supply power for the hangars and outbuildings, with any surplus electricity being sold to the National Grid.

Other former military buildings are being marketed for a variety of purposes, for instance, what is now known as *The Hush House* (once used for testing jet engines and insulated to keep down noise levels) is being offered as an unusual venue for loud music concerts or as a space-age set for film-makers.

There is the well-established Bentwaters Cold War Museum with its static aircraft displays and other memorabilia of the Cold War era, not forgetting that both bases saw action in World War II. This year the museum was successful in obtaining an A10 'Tankbuster' to add to their collection.

The Control Tower has been turned into a very fine meeting place and reception office.

With all the former hangar space Bill can fulfil his ambition to create an 'Agricultural Heritage Centre' to show the history of farming from the days of horse power and steam power all the way through to present day machinery – and show off his collection of 200-plus vintage tractors.

The Air Police HQ building (which replaced the old cottage where my wife and I lived for 13 years) is expected to eventually become a hotel. What a great idea!

Woodbridge, the other Twin Base, remains an active MoD Army camp occupied by the Parachute Regiment (Engineering Section), who recently paraded through the town to celebrate 10 years of being based here. The latest news (2016) is that they are currently creating a temporary runway surface for heavy short takeoff aircraft.

---

[1] Sadly, Linn Barringer died suddenly in 2010 but the website is still up and running and kept going by his daughter.

Epilogue

When the first edition of this book was launched in 2004 I received many compliments about the content and presentation. People seemed to enjoy the fact that it wasn't so much about military operations but instead recorded the development of the Twin Bases through the 50 years they were operational and mentioned some of the memorable people who worked there, both military and civilian.

Many former military personnel in the US were keen to get their hands on a copy of the book and I arranged a mail system through Browser Books. One ex Airman 'Robert' lost his book in a flood and made three attempts to get a replacement.

As I have already mentioned, since 2001 when the first reunion to celebrate the 50th anniversary of the USAF arrival at Bentwaters was held, I have attended several reunions.

The 2016 reunion is due to be held in Washington DC and my daughter Jenny and I will be attending. I look forward to seeing many old friends once again.

Norman Rose *August 2016*